Social Studies Plus!
A Hands-On Approach

Scott
Foresman

Editorial Offices: Glenview, Illinois • Parsippany, New Jersey • New York, New York
Sales Offices: Parsippany, New Jersey • Duluth, Georgia • Glenview, Illinois •
Coppell, Texas • Ontario, California

www.sfsocialstudies.com

Program Authors

Dr. Candy Dawson Boyd
Professor, School of Education
Director of Reading Programs
St. Mary's College
Moraga, California

Dr. Geneva Gay
Professor of Education
University of Washington
Seattle, Washington

Rita Geiger
Director of Social Studies and
    Foreign Languages
Norman Public Schools
Norman, Oklahoma

Dr. James B. Kracht
Associate Dean for
    Undergraduate Programs
    and Teacher Education
College of Education
Texas A&M University
College Station, Texas

Dr. Valerie Ooka Pang
Professor of Teacher Education
San Diego State University
San Diego, California

Dr. C. Frederick Risinger
Director, Professional
    Development and Social
    Studies Education
Indiana University
Bloomington, Indiana

Sara Miranda Sanchez
Elementary and Early
    Childhood Curriculum
    Coordinator
Albuquerque Public Schools
Albuquerque, New Mexico

Contributing Authors

Dr. Carol Berkin
Professor of History
Baruch College and the
    Graduate Center
The City University of New York
New York, New York

Lee A. Chase
Staff Development Specialist
Chesterfield County
    Public Schools
Chesterfield County, Virginia

Dr. Jim Cummins
Professor of Curriculum
Ontario Institute for Studies
    in Education
University of Toronto
Toronto, Canada

Dr. Allen D. Glenn
Professor and Dean Emeritus
Curriculum and Instruction
College of Education
University of Washington
Seattle, Washington

Dr. Carole L. Hahn
Professor, Educational Studies
Emory University
Atlanta, Georgia

Dr. M. Gail Hickey
Professor of Education
Indiana University-Purdue
    University
Fort Wayne, Indiana

Dr. Bonnie Meszaros
Associate Director
Center for Economic Education
    and Entrepreneurship
University of Delaware
Newark, Delaware

ISBN: 0-328-03594-7

Contents

Contents

Welcome to *Social Studies Plus!*

Using Activities to Launch Social Studies Classes

Most educators are all too familiar with the "banking" metaphor of learning, where students sit passively as receivers of information. Educators also know the need to switch that construct to a vital one where students *participate* in the wide world that social studies class can reveal. To jump-start this new metaphor, it helps to have a variety of dynamic and broad-range activities that draw life and direction from the content and skills of basic social studies curriculum. In this way, students begin to realize that the issues of social studies concern things they care about.

Social studies, of course, is about both the forest and the trees. It covers the whole world—big and little events, heroes and ordinary people, issues of justice, morality, and ethics. Social studies is also about the *specific*—the content and skills connected with historical fact and assessing controversial issues that students learn to work with at their own levels of understanding.

When we teach social studies, it is important to join all the important historical, political, and economic aspects of the curriculum with the concrete ways students learn and express themselves. It makes sense, then, to engage students in many different kinds of activities so as to appeal to the varied ways students tackle any curriculum but especially the broad curriculum of social studies. A variety of approaches helps students internalize what citizenship means and how important participation is for a democracy to thrive.

Social Studies Plus! Overview and Purpose

Social Studies Plus! begins with Scott Foresman's social studies basal scope and sequence and then sets up engaging activities that invite students to think independently about events and issues in both the past and present. Some activities create a storytelling atmosphere, where students can move from the concrete to the abstract. Some *Social Studies Plus!* activities place the student in the middle of an historical event and ask the student to take a position and justify it. Other activities promote discussion, questioning, and analysis about the consequences resulting from events, ideas, and persons' actions. Not only should the ideas presented open students' thinking and get them interested in social studies curriculum, the activities should also help students see that they have something at stake in the issues of being a citizen.

Social Studies Plus! offers several approaches in which students may participate:

- Students may create simulations by playing various roles; for instance, they may become members of an immigrant family arriving at Ellis Island, or they may act out the parts of weary soldiers at Valley Forge under General George Washington.

- Students may dig into hands-on activities by drawing themselves on "living" time lines as characters in the early colonies or on the Underground Railroad.

- Students may use their math and graphic organizer skills to map out or graph the fast clip of progress during the Industrial Revolution.

- Students may design labor union broadsides or cartoons about the 1920s, which then may trigger critical discussions of moral and ethical issues.

- Some students may use biographical sketches of famous people in history to stimulate their own writing of persuasive speeches, poems, or news articles that show a variety of perspectives.

Each unit follows a basic progression. First, a Long-Term Project presents a unit theme for students to work on throughout the study of the unit. Second, other unit themes are presented in creative and dramatic form in a six-page Drama section. Third, a number of Short-Term Projects, Writing Projects, and Citizenship activities further develop the topics covered in each chapter.

Read ahead to see how each unit is mapped out and how to make the most of all the projects and activities presented in *Social Studies Plus!*

Long-Term Project

Students are offered a Long-Term Project that may last several days or weeks. The goal of the project is to extend the main ideas of an entire unit and allow students enough time to perform one or several tasks. For instance, students may draw, make graphs, do an interview, or complete some research on one topic. With the Long-Term Project, students have time to enter into the discussion of an issue, or they launch into making something concrete, such as a model, diorama, puppets, and so on. The unit project, then, allows students to integrate key social studies concepts and skills in an organized, and often artistic, way.

These unit-sized projects may suggest that the teacher set the context or recall topics at hand, or the teacher may choose how much background to give students. Students do not always need prior experience with the topics presented. Procedures for handling the project are laid out in easy-to-follow steps where teachers may choose the grouping and specific tasks so that, by unit's end, everyone contributes to an overall display or project. Students usually end up choosing what goes into a report or display, allowing them the chance to *own* a part of the display. One of the most enlightening parts of the unit project happens when students present their endeavors to one another or to other classes. A close second to that experience occurs when their audiences ask the students questions and the students become experts for the moment.

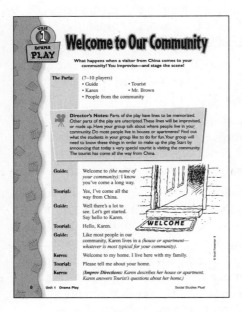

Drama: Plays

Every activity in the Drama section of *Social Studies Plus!* is aimed at creating a dramatic and physical reaction in students to some social studies issues. All the activities give students opportunities for improvising.

The plays are presented either as fully written scripts or as plays with some written lines and suggested ways for improvising additional lines and scenes. In addition, most plays are based on the following parameters:

- The plays take no longer than 30–40 minutes at a time, although play practice and presentation may extend over several class periods.

- The plays are appropriate for each age group in both dialogue and plot complexity.

- The plays are accompanied by a director's guide that will help the student-leader or teacher by providing plot summary, prop and theater term suggestions, or character descriptions.

Drama: Scenarios

Scenarios give students the opportunity to act out brief scenes that draw on their spur-of-the-moment reactions as well as promote their abilities to think on their feet. These scenarios relate to the topics and skills at hand and do not require outside research. Each scenario will:

- provide students with a purpose and focus for the scenario,
- often suggest a conflict relevant to the students' life experiences,
- be easily done in the classroom with a few optional props,
- take only about 10–15 minutes to present,
- and often allow students opportunities to think beyond their usual perspective about facts and people.

There are several common theater terms used throughout the Drama section. See the glossary on page 1 for a full set of theater terms. You may want to copy the page and make it available to the students.

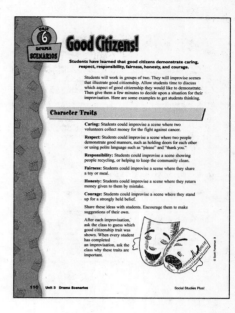

Chapter Development

Short-Term Projects

The goal of the many Short-Term Projects is to extend the chapter content. No projects are repeated from the Teacher's Edition. Rather they proceed from the themes and topics of interest in the Student's Edition and so allow students a myriad of hands-on activities. These projects are oriented toward engaging students in the following ways:

- Short-Term Projects engage small groups, partners, individuals or the whole class in relevant activities.
- They encompass a wide variety of activities: map making, debates, theme mobiles, banners and collages, speeches, time lines from Ancient Egypt to the town of Egypt, Maine, and many more.
- They suggest ways for the students to have fun with social studies topics and skills.
- They cover skills to help students think "out of the box."
- They offer directions that students may follow without much adult assistance.
- They integrate various subject areas into a social studies project.
- They can be completed in about 20–30 minutes.

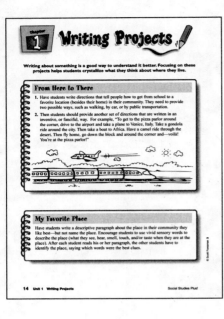

Writing Projects

In a grab bag approach, some Writing Projects allow a wide swath of creativity and some take students through brief, but rigorous, expository writing. The Writing Projects should also include the following goals.

- The Writing Projects engage students in a variety of dynamic writing applications of social studies content and skills and can be completed in about 20–30 minutes.

- They serve as a bridge between students' (a) prior knowledge and life experiences and (b) content of the core text.

- They provide a connection between concrete/operational understanding and the application of social studies concepts/skills to a student's life.

- They should help students experience social studies in ways other than rehashing dates and events.

- They should be intriguing enough to make teachers and students *both* want to try the activities.

Citizenship

Social studies always deals with citizens of the past and present. To show students how important participation is in a democratic society, these activities focus on the traits of a good citizen.

- Each Citizenship page may require some research, creative writing, interviews, or artistic endeavors.

- The goal of this page is to make students more aware of how to spot citizenship traits in their own actions and in the larger neighborhood or community around them.

Blackline Masters

Each chapter has at least one blackline master for students to use to further extend one or more of the activities in the unit or chapter. Some of these pages engage students in crossword puzzles, cartoon strips and storyboards, graphic organizers, map and graph making, and various kinds of artwork.

Assessment for *Social Studies Plus!*

The rubrics suggested for use with *Social Studies Plus!* materials are intended to aid teachers in recording a range of the students' linguistic and cultural experiences.

The emphasis of these rubrics is placed on thinking rather than rote learning, performance and successes rather than failings, and on each individual's development within grade-level expectations. Obviously no rubrics are a substitute for the teacher's classroom observations. A teacher's notes on students' abilities to gain knowledge based on experience is key in helping teachers make students understand what they need to learn.

The rubrics presented in *Social Studies Plus!* pertain to assessing students' achievements while they are engaged in exploring the social studies content and learning new skills. Applying these rubrics to the students' work gives them concrete feedback and helps them monitor their own progress toward meeting performance standards. These rubrics are oriented toward assessing the variety of ways students may approach the content and skills of this program.

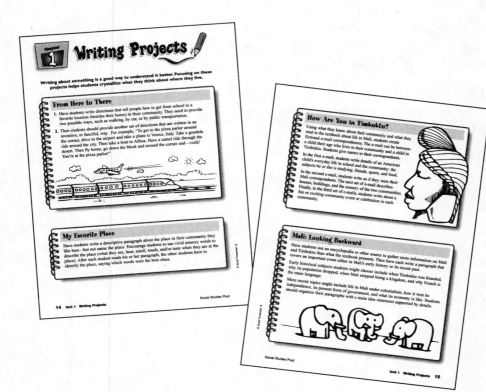

Writing Rubrics

Writing, because it is specific and tangible, may be easier to evaluate than most other subjects. Both analytic and holistic rubrics are used to evaluate writing. Many teachers use holistic scoring because it evaluates a writer's overall ability to express meaning in written form.

Analytic rubrics tend to incorporate spelling, punctuation, and grammar accuracy, yet they also address some complex aspects of writing assessment. This rubric is based on the assumption that teachers will be looking at students' abilities to begin handling some stages of the writing process in relation to social studies content. Once students have some specific ideas of how to improve their writing, they can begin to be their own editors.

4-point rubric

4 Excellent   **3** Very Good   **2** Satisfactory   **1** Needs Improvement

Six Traits for the Analytic Writing Rubric

Content Quality and Idea Development

genre well controlled, interesting, clear, complex, organized, details in place

Voice

specific, honest, appealing, clear point of view, appropriate use of action verbs, easy to follow

Organization

complete text, details in place, smooth transitions, fluency of thought, builds anticipation, creates interest, contains beginning, middle, and end

Word Precision

interesting, precise, and vivid word choice, strong verbs, understands appropriate phrasing, handles repairs well

Sentence Fluency

variation in sentence structure and length, uses sentence patterns when appropriate

Mechanics

correct grammar and spelling, sensible paragraphing, formal and informal punctuation used appropriately, easy to read

Rubric for Narrative Writing

	4 Excellent	3 Very Good	2 Satisfactory	1 Needs Improvement
Content Quality and Idea Development	• well-developed story • well-focused on the topic • clear ideas are well-supported with interesting and vivid details	• fairly well-developed story • focused on the topic • ideas are well-supported with details	• sometimes strays from topic • ideas are not well-developed • more details are needed	• poorly focused on the topic • ideas are unclear • few details are given
Voice	• voice is fitting for the topic and engaging • well-suited for audience and purpose	• voice is fairly clear and seems to fit the topic • suited for audience and purpose	• voice rarely comes through • not always suited for audience and purpose	• voice is weak or inappropriate • no sense of audience or purpose
Organization	• well-focused on the topic • logical organization • sequence is very clear • excellent transitions • easy to follow	• generally focused on the topic • some lapses in organization • has a beginning, middle, and end • some transitions • usually easy to follow	• somewhat focused on the topic • poor organization and some difficulty with sequence • few transitions • difficult to follow	• not focused on the topic • no clear organization • no clear sequence • difficult to impossible to follow
Word Precision	• precise, vivid, and interesting word choices • wide variety of word choices	• fairly precise, interesting, and somewhat varied word choices • wording could be more specific	• vague, mundane word choices • wording is sometimes repetitive • more descriptive words are needed	• very limited word choices • wording is bland and not descriptive
Sentence Fluency	• uses complete sentences • varying sentence structures and lengths	• uses complete sentences • generally simple sentence structures	• occasional sentence fragment or run-on sentence • simple sentence structure is used repeatedly	• frequent use of sentence fragments or run-on sentences • sentences are difficult to understand
Mechanics	• proper grammar and usage • correct spelling • correct punctuation • correct capitalization	• few errors of grammar and usage • mostly correct spelling, punctuation, and capitalization	• errors in grammar, usage, and spelling sometimes make understanding difficult • some errors in punctuation and capitalization	• frequent errors in grammar, usage, spelling, capitalization, and punctuation make understanding difficult or impossible

Rubric for Persuasive Writing

	4 Excellent	3 Very Good	2 Satisfactory	1 Needs Improvement
Content Quality and Idea Development	• clear position is well-supported and insightful • complete control of topic • many facts and opinions to support position • presents a convincing argument	• clear position is somewhat supported • good control of topic • some facts and opinions to support position • presents a fairly convincing argument	• position is taken, but not supported • some control of topic • few facts and opinions to support position • presents a weak argument	• no clear position taken • little control of topic • no facts and opinions given • no argument presented
Voice	• voice is strong and engaging • specific, honest, engaging point of view • well-suited for audience and purpose	• voice is fairly strong • generally clear, honest, engaging point of view • suited for audience and purpose	• voice rarely comes through • general, vague discussion of topic • not always suited for audience and purpose	• voice is weak or inappropriate • no particular point of view presented • no sense of audience of purpose
Organization	• well-focused on the topic • logical organization with reasons presented in a clear order • contains beginning, middle, and end • easy to follow argument	• generally focused on the topic • organization is mostly clear but reasons not always presented in a clear order • contains beginning, middle, and end • usually easy to follow argument	• somewhat focused on the topic • poor organization with only a few reasons presented • no clear beginning, middle, and end • difficult to follow argument	• not focused on the topic • no clear organization • no reasons presented • no clear beginning, middle, and end • no argument presented
Word Precision	• precise, persuasive word choices • interesting word choice • fluency of thought • appropriate use of action verbs	• fairly precise, persuasive word choices • wording could be more specific • generally appropriate use of action verbs	• vague, unpersuasive word choices • wording is general and not convincing • wording is sometimes repetitive	• very limited word choices • fails to persuade • wording is redundant and bland
Sentence Fluency	• uses complete sentences • varying sentence structures and lengths	• uses complete sentences • generally simple sentence structures	• occasional sentence fragment or run-on sentence • simple sentence structure is used repeatedly	• frequent use of sentence fragments or run-on sentences • sentences are difficult to understand
Mechanics	• proper grammar and usage • correct spelling • correct punctuation • correct capitalization	• few errors of grammar and usage • mostly correct spelling, punctuation, and capitalization	• errors in grammar, usage, and spelling sometimes make understanding difficult • some errors in punctuation and capitalization	• frequent errors in grammar, usage, spelling, capitalization, and punctuation make understanding difficult or impossible

Rubric for Expressive/Descriptive Writing

	4 Excellent	3 Very Good	2 Satisfactory	1 Needs Improvement
Content Quality and Idea Development	• "paints a picture" for the reader • well-focused on the topic • clear ideas are well-supported with interesting and vivid details	• creates some clear images for the reader • focused on the topic • ideas are well-supported with details	• sometimes strays from topic • ideas are not well-developed • more details are needed	• poorly focused on the topic • ideas are unclear • few details are given
Voice	• voice is fitting for the topic and engaging • well-suited for audience and purpose	• voice is fairly clear and seems to fit the topic • suited for audience and purpose	• voice rarely comes through • not always suited for audience and purpose	• voice is weak or inappropriate • no sense of audience or purpose
Organization	• well focused on the topic • logical organization • excellent transitions • easy to follow	• generally focused on the topic • some lapses in organization • some transitions • usually easy to follow	• somewhat focused on the topic • poor organization • few transitions • difficult to follow	• not focused on the topic • no clear organization • no transitions • difficult to impossible to follow
Word Precision	• precise, vivid, and interesting word choices • wide variety of word choices	• fairly precise, interesting, and somewhat varied word choices • wording could be more specific	• vague, mundane word choices • wording is sometimes repetitive • more descriptive words are needed	• very limited word choices • wording is bland and not descriptive
Sentence Fluency	• uses complete sentences • varying sentence structures and lengths	• uses complete sentences • generally simple sentence structures	• occasional sentence fragment or run-on sentence • simple sentence structure is used repeatedly	• frequent use of sentence fragments or run-on sentences • sentences are difficult to understand
Mechanics	• proper grammar and usage • correct spelling • correct punctuation • correct capitalization	• few errors of grammar and usage • mostly correct spelling, punctuation, and capitalization	• errors in grammar, usage, and spelling sometimes make understanding difficult • some errors in punctuation and capitalization	• frequent errors in grammar, usage, spelling, capitalization, and punctuation make understanding difficult or impossible

Rubric for Expository Writing

	4 Excellent	3 Very Good	2 Satisfactory	1 Needs Improvement
Content Quality and Idea Development	• well-focused on the topic • clear ideas are well-supported with interesting details	• focused on the topic • ideas are well-supported with details	• sometimes strays from topic • ideas are not well-developed • more details are needed	• poorly focused on the topic • ideas are unclear • few details are given
Voice	• voice is strong and engaging • well-suited for audience and purpose	• voice is fairly strong • suited for audience and purpose	• voice rarely comes through • not always suited for audience and purpose	• voice is weak or inappropriate • no sense of audience or purpose
Organization	• well-focused on the topic • logical organization • excellent transitions • easy to follow	• generally focused on the topic • organization is mostly clear • some transitions • usually easy to follow	• somewhat focused on the topic • poor organization • few transitions • difficult to follow	• not focused on the topic • no clear organization • no transitions • difficult to impossible to follow
Word Precision	• precise, interesting word choices • wide variety of word choices	• fairly precise, interesting word choices • wording could be more specific	• vague, mundane word choices • wording is sometimes repetitive	• very limited word choices • wording is bland
Sentence Fluency	• strong topic sentence • varying sentence structures and lengths • uses complete sentences	• good topic sentence • generally simple sentence structures • uses complete sentences	• weak topic sentence • simple sentence structure is used repeatedly • occasional sentence fragment or run-on sentence	• no topic sentence • sentences are difficult to understand • frequent use of sentence fragments or run-on sentences
Mechanics	• proper grammar and usage • correct spelling • correct punctuation • correct capitalization	• few errors of grammar and usage • mostly correct spelling, punctuation, and capitalization	• errors in grammar, usage, and spelling sometimes make understanding difficult • some errors in punctuation and capitalization	• frequent errors in grammar, usage, spelling, capitalization, and punctuation make understanding difficult or impossible

Class Projects Rubric

Social Studies Plus! presents numerous projects, for both individual and group work, making the rubric for the elements of content and skill more general. Many of the students' products resulting from these projects may be assessed as well by placing some in student portfolios or displaying them in the classroom. The rubric below is a general guide for assessing the projects.

Individual/Collaborative Projects

Directions: Copy the rubric for either groups or individuals. Circle the appropriate number for individual and collaborative participation in the projects.

Skill/Performance	Excellent	Very Good	Satisfactory	Needs Improvement
1. Collaborative reading/ understand task	4	3	2	1
2. Group listens to group leader	4	3	2	1
3. Group members listen to one another	4	3	2	1
4. Group understands cross-curricular skills needed	4	3	2	1
5. Group designs and constructs project in organized way	4	3	2	1
6. Individual uses right skills for environmental and historical research	4	3	2	1
7. Individual plans and executes art/craft project	4	3	2	1
8. Individual uses prior knowledge to complete task	4	3	2	1
9. Individual uses skill strategies, such as comparison, analysis, outlining, and map reading to complete task	4	3	2	1
10. Individual shows ability to reflect on what is the topic and what is important	4	3	2	1

Drama Rubric

Directions: Make a form for each student. Circle the appropriate number for each individual's participation in the play or scenario.

Student Name: _____

Skill/Performance	Excellent	Very Good	Satisfactory	Needs Improvement
1. Understands task	4	3	2	1
2. Plans own part	4	3	2	1
3. Understands the movement in front of group; maintains eye contact	4	3	2	1
4. Researched and practiced part	4	3	2	1
5. Willing to improvise in context	4	3	2	1
6. Projection and diction	4	3	2	1
7. Concentration and poise in acting	4	3	2	1
8. Language clear and delivered with enthusiasm	4	3	2	1
9. Understood content correctly	4	3	2	1
10. Delivered in believable way	4	3	2	1

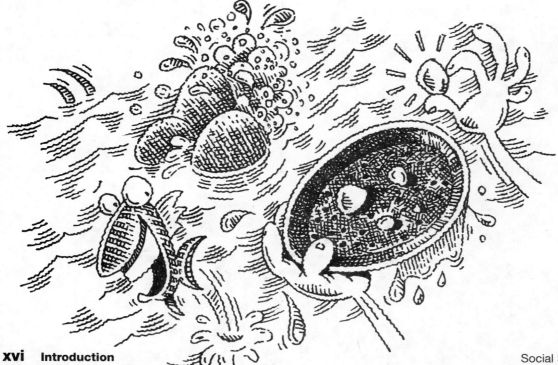

Glossary of Theater Terms

backdrop: a painting that shows the setting for a play; it hangs at the back of the stage, and scenes are played in front of it

blocking: setting the actors' positions and moves during rehearsal

center stage: in the middle of the stage

cue: a signal (a word, phrase, sound, or other action) to an actor or actors to enter, exit, or to begin a speech or action

downstage: the part of the stage that is nearest the audience

enter: to come onto the stage from the wings

exit: to leave the stage

Improv Directions: instructions for actors about moments when they must make up lines or actions

improvise: when actors make up material on the spot or in rehearsal

mime: a form of acting in which actions are used without words

monologue: a speech by one person

pantomime: the silent telling of a story through gestures, body movements, and facial expressions

pre-set: the set-up of the stage that is in place as the play begins

prologue: a short scene that comes before the main body of a play and introduces the theme

prop: any item needed by actors that they can carry on and off stage

ritual: a set of actions with special significance for the community, performed in a formal, stylized way

role-play: to improvise a character in a given situation

scene titles: signs written in large letters for the audience to read, announcing the titles of scenes

script: the written text of a play

scripted: written down, when all the lines are on the page

setting: when and where the action of a play occurs

stage directions: directions to the actors, usually in parentheses

stage right: the right-hand side from the actor's point of view, onstage, facing the audience

stage left: the left-hand side from the actor's point of view, onstage, facing the audience

tableau vivant or tableau: literally, a living picture; a scene where actors freeze to form a picture

unscripted: parts of a play that are not written down, where the actor(s) must improvise

upstage: relating to the rear of the stage

Long-Term Project pages 4–5	Materials	🕐	Lesson Link
Sell That Community: The Brochure Way Students create brochures that will convince people to live in certain communities.			Lessons 1–3
Week 1 ♦♦♦ **group** Students research different communities, and choose one they would like to create a brochure about.	brochures for reference, library resources, map	1 session 30 min.	
Week 2 ♦♦♦ **group** Students select members for research, writing, and drawing assignments for the brochures.	pencils, pens, paper, computer (word-processing program), printer	1 session 45–60 min	
Week 3 ♦♦♦ **group** Students establish layout of text and pictures for their brochures.	paper, colored pencils, markers, rulers, scissors, photos, tape or paste	1 session 1–1$\frac{1}{2}$ hrs.	
Unit Drama pages 6–11			
Scenarios: Act it Out! ♦♦♦ **group** Students hone their improvisation skills by pantomiming and playing charades.	props and costumes (optional)	2 sessions 20 min. each	Lesson 1
Play: Welcome to Our Community ♦♦♦ **group** Students perform a play about a person from China visiting the community.	props and costumes (optional)	1 session 30 min.	Lesson 1
One Moon Above Us ♦♦♦ **group** Students perform a play about living in the city, the suburbs, and the country.	props and costumes (optional)	1 session 25 min.	Lesson 2
Chapter 1 Short-Term Projects pages 12–13			
Community Flag or Seal ♦♦♦ **group** Students design flags or seals to represent their community.	pens or markers, construction paper, oaktag or cardboard	1 session 20 min.	Lesson 1
A Long, Long Way from Home ♦♦♦ **group** Students use a road mileage chart to calculate the distance between their community and other cities.	magazines, construction paper, various art supplies	1 session 30 min.	Lesson 2
Community Motto ♦♦♦ **group** Students make up a motto to describe the community in which they live.	magazines, construction paper, various art supplies	1 session 15 min.	Lesson 2
More "Official" Community Items ♦♦♦ **group** Students make illustrated charts for a community reference book.	pens or markers, construction paper, oaktag	1 session 20 min.	Lesson 2
Eye-catchers ♦♦♦ **group** Students create pictures of eye-catchers found in their community, emphasizing what makes them special.	pens or markers, oaktag, craft sticks, string, tape, scissors	1 session 15 min.	Lesson 2

Chapter 1 **Writing Projects** pages 14–15	Materials	⏱	Lesson Link
From Here to There 🧍 individual Students write directions telling how to get from school to a favorite location.	paper, pencils	1 session 20 min.	Lesson 1
My Favorite Place 🧍 individual Students write descriptive paragraphs about a favorite place in their community.	paper, pencils	1 session 15 min.	Lesson 1
How are You in Timbuktu? 🧍 individual Students create fictional e-mail correspondences with a student in Mali.	paper, pencils	1 session 20 min.	Lesson 3
Mali: Looking Backward 🧍 individual Students write paragraphs about an important event either in Mali's history or its recent past.	paper, pencils, reference material on Mali	1 session 25 min.	Lesson 3

Chapter 1 **Citizenship Project** page 16			
Caring 🧍🧍🧍 group Students brainstorm community organizations and make a list of programs they would like to be involved in.	paper, pencils, BLM p. 17	1 session 1 hr.	Lessons 1–3

Chapter 2 **Short-Term Projects** pages 18–19			
Welcome, Stranger—Welcome Home 🧍 individual Students design welcome signs to be posted at the boundary of the community.	pens or markers, construction paper, oaktag or cardboard	1 session 20 min.	Lessons 1–3
When Did Everyone Get Here? 🧍 individual Students use a population graph to answer questions about the community's population.	BLM p. 23, pencil, ruler	1 session 30 min.	Lessons 1–3
"Raise High the Roof Beams" 🧍🧍🧍 group Students make models of buildings in the community.	shoe boxes, various art supplies	1 session 45 min.	Lessons 1–3
Past and Present 🧍 individual Students paint or draw their own versions of how the land shapes of their areas may have looked in previous times.	watercolors, colored pencils or markers, construction paper	1 session 30 min.	Lessons 1–3
The Future 🧍🧍 partners Students draw pictures of what they think their community will look like in 2500.	watercolors, colored pencils or markers, construction paper	1 session 40 min.	Lessons 1–3

Chapter 2 **Writing Projects** pages 20–21			
Have a Nice Day 🧍 individual Students write about living in a different kind of community.	paper, pencils	1 session 20 min.	Lessons 1–3
Hear Ye, Hear Ye 🧍 individual Students write newspaper announcements about a particular event they wish the community sponsored.	paper, pencils	1 session 15 min.	Lessons 1–3

Chapter **2** Writing Projects *continued*	Materials	⏱	Lesson Link
In Honor of . . . ⚇ **individual** Students write poems honoring someone from their community.	paper, pencils	1 session 25 min.	Lessons 1–3
You're Invited ⚇ **individual** Students write a letter to a well-known organization, inviting it to hold its next gathering in their community.	paper, pencils	1 session 20 min.	Lessons 1–3
Destination: Tokyo ⚇ **individual** Students practice setting up a friendly letter to someone from a foreign community.	paper, pencils	1 session 25 min.	Lessons 1–3
Chapter **2** Citizenship Project page 22			
Responsibility ⚇⚇⚇ **group** Students play a game called Community Advertising Responsibility.	pencils, index cards	1 session 45 min.	Lessons 1–3

NOTES

Long-Term Project

Sell That Community: The Brochure Way

Your students probably have ideas about what makes a community a great place to live. Invite them to create brochures that will convince people to visit or live in certain communities.

Advance Preparation: *The purpose of this project is to create promotional brochures that highlight the unique qualities of a community as an urban, suburban, or rural place. The target audience is people looking for a specific kind of community to visit or to call home. The brochure may be displayed in a central area of the school or in the classroom—similar to ways that chambers of commerce might display brochures.*

If it's possible to prepare ahead of time, make up two ways to fold or arrange paper for the brochures. Have the two models on hand. (For example, show students how to fold the large piece of paper into the panels of a brochure or, for the second model, show them how to organize the material into several sheets of paper.)

Research

Week 1

♟♟ group   ⏱ 30 minutes

Materials: brochure models, library and local resources, map

Students work in groups to develop brochures about different aspects of a community. Each group chooses a different community. The community of choice can be a part of the city, region, or state that the group knows. It can also be a place students have always wanted to know about and visit. Make sure that no two groups choose the same community. The students' research involves learning how to distinguish between important and unimportant information. They work together to present their information in an appealing way.

Week 2

Write It Up

Materials: pencils, pens, paper, computer with word-processing program and printer

Explain to students that each member of a group will do the research, writing, pictures, and design for one subject or aspect of the group's community. These aspects may include landmarks, houses, indoor recreation, outdoor recreation, or other subjects, depending on what the community offers. Each student is responsible for deciding what aspects are important enough to be included in the brochure. While groups are working, circulate among them to answer questions and offer tips.

Week 3

Bring It Together

Materials: paper, colored pencils, markers, rulers, scissors, photos, tape or paste

Step 1: Offer students a choice between one large piece of paper or several 8½ x11 inch sheets of paper for their brochures. Have on hand the two kinds of model brochures you have made up ahead of time. These models will give students a guide for organizing their written material. Help students allow room for writing and pictures. Artwork can be illustrations, photos, or a combination of the two. Students should do as much of their own work as possible, but help them to organize their material to make it attractive and easy to read.

Step 2: After students have selected the photos and done the planning for the brochure, they should write captions for the photos. Help them make layouts for their sections of the brochure. Give each picture and text the room it needs, and arrange the elements to fit the pages.

Act It Out!

It's good to warm up before a play by doing some pantomimes. Loosen up and have some fun snapping live pictures and playing charades.

Scenario 1: Snapshot

Say cheese! Communities are great places to photograph people working and playing. In this theater game you will act as if you are "snapping" some great pictures. Divide into group of four or five students each.

First, think about places you go in your community. Libraries, supermarkets, and parks are some suggestions. One student in each group acts as the photographer.

The photographer poses the other students who pantomime an activity in one of your locations. For example, in a supermarket, students could mime taking groceries off shelves. They could push shopping carts. When the photographer is ready to take the picture, she or he calls out "freeze." The rest of the class tries to guess where the picture is set.

If possible, invite the photographer to take an actual photograph of each community scene, using an instant camera you have provided. Once the photographs have been developed, ask the students to organize them on a classroom bulletin board labeled "Charades Snapshots."

Scenario 2: A Game of Charades

Rules and Lists

Most everyone has played charades and knows that one person acts out the name of a person, place, thing, or expression while another person or group guesses what is being acted out. In this game of charades, act out the different jobs of people who work in your community.

To help you think up ideas, here are some things to talk about:
Who takes care of your community park?
Who takes care of the injured and sick?
Who cares for you when your parents are away from home?
Who makes sure your community is safe?
Who takes care of leaks in your faucets?
Who fights fires in your community?

Write each job on a separate index card, shuffle the deck, and place it facedown. Have a volunteer demonstrate some charades techniques: how to indicate "break up a word into parts"; how to indicate "sounds like" or how to show when you are acting out a "whole idea."

Playing the Game

Remember that it is fun to act out the job or person in exaggerated ways. When the class is divided into two group, one group starts by drawing a card and acting out the job. The other group has to guess the job. Decide on a time limit of around three minutes. Have fun watching your classmates pantomime, and guessing jobs and people from your community.

KEEP OUR COMMUNITY CLEAN

Welcome to Our Community

What happens when a visitor from China comes to your community? You improvise—and stage the scene!

The Parts: (7–10 players)
- Guide
- Tourist
- Karen
- Mr. Brown
- People from the community

Director's Notes: Parts of the play have lines to be memorized. Other parts of the play are unscripted. These lines will be improvised, or made up. Have your group talk about where people live in your community. Do most people live in houses or apartments? Find out what the students in your group like to do for fun. Your group will need to know these things in order to make up the play. Start by announcing that today a very special tourist is visiting the community. The tourist has come all the way from China.

Guide: Welcome to *(the name of your community)*. I know you've come a long way.

Tourist: Yes, I've come all the way from China.

Guide: Well there's a lot to see. Let's get started. Say hello to Karen.

Tourist: Hello, Karen.

Guide: Like most people in our community, Karen lives in a *(house or apartment— whatever is most typical for your community)*.

Karen: Welcome to my home. I live here with my family.

Tourist: Please tell me about your home.

Karen: *(Improv Directions: Karen describes her house or apartment. Karen answers Tourist's questions about her home.)*

Tourist:	Your home is very nice.
Karen:	Thank you. Good-bye. *(Exits.)*
Guide:	Have you eaten yet?
Tourist:	Just a little something on the plane.
Guide:	Then you must be hungry. We'll go to my favorite restaurant. People come from far away just to eat there.
Mr. Brown:	*(entering)* Welcome to my restaurant.
Guide:	Hello, Mr. Brown. This is my friend.
Tourist:	Hello, what is good to eat here?
Mr. Brown:	*(**Improv Directions:** Mr. Brown answers Tourist's questions about the food. Tourist and Guide order lunch. Mr. Brown serves them and exits.)*
Tourist:	That was delicious.
Guide:	I hope you're not tired. There's one more place I'd like to take you.
Tourist:	Where are we going?
Guide:	Where kids go to have a good time.
Tourist:	What is this place?
Guide:	Why don't you ask someone? *(Two or three people enter.)*
Tourist:	Excuse me, what are you doing?
People:	*(**Improv Directions:** The people answer the Tourist.)*
Tourist:	That looks like fun. I wish I could do that.
Person:	It's easy to do. We'll teach you. *(**Improv Directions:** They teach Tourist how to play.)*
Tourist:	What a wonderful day. Thank you for showing me your community.
Guide:	We hope you'll come back soon.
Tourist:	And I hope you will visit my community in China.
Guide:	That would be great! Good-bye. So long.

Theater Talk

To **enter** is to come onstage. To **exit** is to leave the stage.

One Moon Above Us—A Play

What would it be like to live in the city, the country, or the suburbs? With friends in each community it's easy to find out!

The Parts: (3 players) • Maria
• John • Nancy

📽️ **Director's Notes:** Divide the classroom stage area into stage right, center stage, and stage left. John stands in the stage right area. Maria stands in the stage left area. Nancy stands center stage. Tell the actors to face the audience as they speak their lines. The stage directions are in parentheses.

(John, Nancy, and Maria take their places stage right, center stage, and stage left. They look at their watches.)

John: Three.

Nancy: Two.

Maria: One.

All Three: Now!

John: *(looking at the audience)* Hi, Maria. Hi, Nancy.

Nancy: *(looking at the audience)* Hi, John. Hi, Maria.

Maria: *(looking at the audience)* Hi, John. Hi, Nancy.

John: I'm out in the field behind the barn.

Maria: I'm on the roof of my apartment building.

Nancy: I'm in the backyard.

John: It's quiet here. The only sounds are the cows mooing.

Nancy: I can hear the clink of knives and forks against plates. The neighbors are eating dinner.

> **Theater Talk**
>
> **Stage right** is the right side of the stage when the actor is facing the audience. **Center stage** is the middle of the stage. **Stage left** is the left side of the stage when the actor is facing the audience.

Maria:	There are lots of cars and buses on the street below. I hear car horns beeping and brakes screeching.
John:	What did you do today?
Nancy:	My mom drove me to school before she took the train to work in the city.
John:	I got up early to feed the chickens. Then I took the bus to school.
Maria:	I took the subway to school. We're learning how to read maps.
Nancy:	We're learning about communities. Did you know that some people travel on camels in Timbuktu? That's in West Africa.
Maria:	I can use a map scale to find out how many miles there are between Nancy's home in the suburbs and John's home in the country.
John:	After school I went to a meeting of the 4-H Club.
Nancy:	A friend's mother drove us to the mall.
Maria:	My dad took me to a museum.
John:	In the 4-H Club we learn about plants and animals. It's fun.
Nancy:	I bought some school supplies. Then we had pizza.
Maria:	I saw a lot of paintings. One looked like John's farm.
Nancy:	Boy, did we have fun there last summer. I miss you guys.
John:	I miss you guys too.
Maria:	Guess what! My mom is going to let me visit you.
John:	I can't wait.
Maria:	*(looking up)* Wow, look, guys. The moon is rising up over the buildings.
John:	*(looking up)* It's rising over the fields in the country.
Nancy:	*(looking up)* It's rising over the houses in the suburbs.
John:	I know we're not together right now. We're in different places.
Maria:	But it's nice to know we're looking at the same moon.

Short-Term Projects

States have flags and seals, mottoes, birds, and other "official" emblems. So why not your community? Read on for some projects in which students can capture the spirit of their community.

Community Flag or Seal

👥👥 group   🕐 20 minutes

Materials: pens or markers; construction paper, oaktag, or cardboard

The designs of state flags and seals often have historical significance or embody a principle that captures a state's spirit. Communities also have historical significance and/or a spirit worth picturing on a flag or a seal. Students should work in groups of two to four and talk about events or places they know are unique to their state. They might like to vote for the best idea and make a rough design for a flag or seal. Finally, have students work on a color version. You may want to laminate the finished flags and seals. Hang them on your "Community" bulletin board.

A Long, Long Way from Home

👥👥 group   🕐 30 minutes

Materials: pens or markers; magazines; scissors; paste; construction paper, oaktag, or cardboard

Guideposts were often used at crossroads, and still are, to show distances to nearby towns. Have students imagine that their community is at the center of the world, with guideposts at its main intersection showing distances to well-known destinations. Have them select a half dozen, such as New York, Dallas, Washington DC, San Francisco, Chicago, and Seattle.

Have students use a road mileage chart similar to one found in an atlas. If their community is on the chart, they can find the mileage by using the vertical and horizontal lines. If the community is not on the chart, they need to use the distance from their community to a nearby city that is on the chart. Then they should add or subtract the distance between their community and that city. This method won't give the exact mileage, but it will be approximate. Have each group write the distances on their guideposts. Then have them put guideposts together with string or heavy tape so that each one points in the general direction of the location it announces.

Community Motto

♟♟ group   ⏰ **15 minutes**

Materials: colored pencils or markers, magazines, scissors, paste, construction paper or oaktag

Working in the same or different groups as the first two activities, students come up with a motto that reflects the best of what their community offers. Give students examples of mottoes you or the students might know. For example, the Boy Scouts motto is "Be Prepared"; advertisers have created the motto "We Try Harder" for a car rental company. Help students to list descriptive words about state places, people, or ideas they have been talking about. Any motto should be short (fewer than ten words) and does not have to contain the community name.

BE PREPARED

More "Official" Community Items

♟♟ group   ⏰ **20 minutes**

Materials: pens or markers; construction paper, oaktag, or cardboard

Working in the same or different groups as in the other activities, students make a chart illustrated with drawings or cutout photographs for a community reference book. Decide on a size for the pages. They can be a full 8½-by-11 inches or smaller. Suggest students use one page for each item. The categories for the chart are "official" community items such as trees, flowers, animals, sports, colors, food, and so on. Categories and entries can run from the serious to the silly.

Remember! Keep working on that Long-Term Project.

Eye-catchers

♟♟ group   ⏰ **15 minutes**

Materials: pens or markers, oaktag, craft sticks, string, tape, scissors

Have students think of something they pass on their way to school that really grabs their eye. It could be a house, a tree, a store, a monument, a person, a sign, or anything else. Announce this activity in advance so students can observe carefully. Have each student create a picture of an eye-catcher in its surroundings, emphasizing what makes it special. When students are finished, display the eye-catchers and have other students from the class try to identify them.

Writing Projects

Writing about something is a good way to understand it better. Focusing on these projects helps students crystallize what they think about where they live.

From Here to There

1. Have students write directions that tell people how to get from school to a favorite location (besides their home) in their community. They need to provide two possible ways, such as walking, by car, or by public transportation.

2. Then students should provide another set of directions that are written in an inventive, or fanciful, way. For example, "To get to the pizza parlor around the corner, drive to the airport and take a plane to Venice, Italy. Take a gondola ride around the city. Then take a boat to Africa. Have a camel ride through the desert. Then fly home, go down the block and around the corner and—voilà! You're at the pizza parlor!"

My Favorite Place

Have students write a descriptive paragraph about the place in their community they like best—but not name the place. Encourage students to use vivid sensory words to describe the place (what they see, hear, smell, touch, and/or taste when they are at the place). After each student reads his or her paragraph, the other students have to identify the place, saying which words were the best clues.

How Are You in Timbuktu?

Using what they know about their community and what they read in the textbook about life in Mali, students create fictional e-mail correspondences. The e-mail can be between a child their age who lives in their community and a child in Timbuktu. Students give names to their correspondents.

In the first e-mail, students write details of an American child's everyday life in school and the community: the subjects he or she is studying, friends, sports, and food.

In the second e-mail, students write as if they were their Mali correspondents. The next set of e-mail describes houses, buildings, and the scenery of the two communities. Finally, in the third set of e-mails, students write about a fun or exciting community event or celebration in each community.

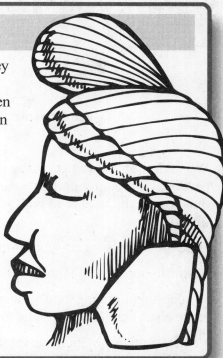

Mali: Looking Backward

Have students use an encyclopedia or other source to gather more information on Mali and Timbuktu than what the textbook presents. Then have each write a paragraph that covers an important event either in Mali's early history or its recent past.

Early historical subjects students might choose include when Timbuktu was founded, why its population dropped, when Mali stopped being a kingdom, and why French is the main language.

More recent topics might include life in Mali under colonialism, how it won its independence, its present form of government, and what its economy is like. Students should organize their paragraphs with a main idea statement supported by details.

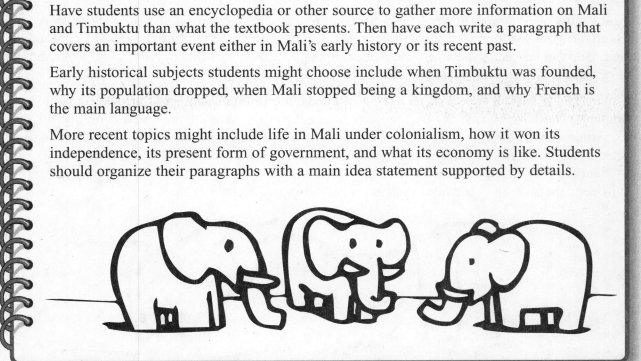

Citizenship

Caring

Talking about caring in a community is the first step toward action. Doing a project is the next step. And finally, results!

What kind of helping or caring programs exist in your community that your students can take part in? Find out by doing research in the phone book and in community information brochures that you might be able to pick up from your local government, chamber of commerce, or public library.

Here are some suggestions for programs that some communities have:

• tutoring or playing with a younger child

• "adopting a grandparent"—terrific for children whose grandparents live elsewhere (and for older adults whose grandchildren live elsewhere)

• entertaining or helping serve at a nursing home

• planting a community garden

• cleaning up a neglected outdoor lot

• writing to members of the armed forces

• making things for a fund-raising bazaar

• getting involved with an organized service club

Make a list of programs that exist in your community and other programs you wish existed. Hand out your list to students and suggest they spend some time looking it over. Then reproduce and hand out copies of the blackline master on page 17. Ask students to fill it out. Tell students they can substitute their own ideas if they like.

Collect the filled-out sheets. Organize the students into groups. Hand out the sheets again. For students who have chosen existing projects, make sure they have the information on how to join. For students who have chosen projects that are not in existence, have them use the ideas on their sheets to brainstorm how they can begin to participate in their project. Discuss ideas with students in each group and give them suggestions on how to get started. Mention that students will need their parents' permission to get involved in any activity.

My Citizenship Project

Which project interests you most? (Or suggest one of your own.)

_____

Why does this project interest you?

_____

_____

_____

Is it a project that exists?

Yes _____   No _____

Draw a picture here of you doing your project.

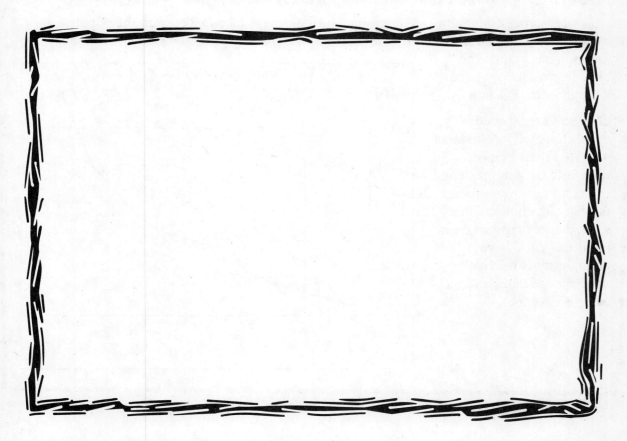

Chapter 2 Short-Term Projects

Communities grow and change over time. Take your students on
a graphic and pictorial tour through old and new changes.

Welcome, Stranger–Welcome Home 👤 individual 🕐 20 minutes

Materials: pens or markers; construction paper, oaktag, or cardboard

Many communities have signs posted along roads at their town or city limits that welcome
motorists and pedestrians. Some are advertisements for places up ahead. But others make
you feel welcome. Have students design a welcome sign to be posted at the boundary of
your community, to *welcome* people. The sign should be easy to see, lively, and get the
message across to both strangers and residents that the community is glad to have
visitors—passing through or coming to stay a while.

When Did Everyone Get Here? 👤 individual 🕐 30 minutes

Materials: copy of blackline master (page 23), pencil, ruler

How old is your community? When was the first census taken? Research the population
statistics of your community. Provide population figures from which students can make a
line or a bar graph. The
blackline master on page
23 goes with this activity.

Choose years spaced
proportionately so students
will find their graphs
relatively easy to make and
to read. If your community
is very old, choose dates
spaced every fifty or even
hundred years. If your
community is relatively
new, choose dates spaced
every ten years.

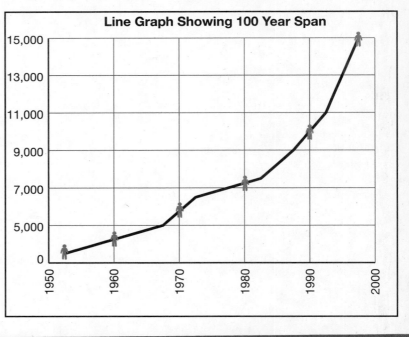

"Raise High the Roof Beams"

group **45 minutes**

Materials: pens, colored pencils, or markers; oaktag or cardboard; paste or tape; shoe boxes or similar diorama materials (optional)

Students work in groups, making models of buildings in their community. As preparation for this activity, gather pictures of buildings from newspapers and magazines. Or, ask students to bring in photographs they may have of their neighborhoods.

Step 1. Make a list for students of how buildings differ: for example, materials (brick, stone, wood), styles (colonial, modern), shapes (one-story "ranch," split-level, many stories), arrangements (attached, semi-attached, detached), and details (windows, balconies, roof shape).

Step 2. Ask students to focus on what makes a building stand out from the others around it.

Step 3. Each group of students will choose one building to work on. It can be a house, a store, or a public building. The building can stand alone or inside a diorama.

Step 4. Display the buildings on a table or in your school's display space.

Past and Present

individual **30 minutes**

Materials: watercolors, colored pencils, or markers; construction paper

Perhaps your students take for granted how your community looks today. You may be able to find pictures of your community before much building was done. What was there beforehand? Forests, open fields, a desert, a swamp? If you're unable to find a single picture, you can probably find a written description. Have students paint or draw their own versions of how the land shapes of their areas may have looked in previous times.

Remember! Keep working on that Long-Term Project.

The Future

partners **40 minutes**

Materials: watercolors, colored pencils, or markers; construction paper

To go with their "before" picture, have students paint or draw a fanciful "after" picture of their community in the year 2500. Have them think before they start: Will people look the same or different? What will they be wearing? What will they be riding around in? To extend these two activities, make cardboard or construction paper frames for both the "before" and "after" pictures.

Writing Projects

Have a Nice Day

Students imagine they live in a community that's different from the one in which they live. For example, if they live in an urban community, they imagine living in a suburban or rural community. Their task is to write about living in a different kind of community. Ask students to imagine going to a birthday party, a public park, or a bike ride in this unfamiliar setting. Would some things be the same? What would be different? Encourage them to explain.

Hear Ye, Hear Ye

Ask students to think of a community event—or one they wished the community had. It can be a serious one such as a parade to honor veterans, or a funny one such as a community-wide pie-eating contest. Have each student write a newspaper announcement for the event. It can be a short blurb or a large display ad. Encourage students to use words that motivate everyone in the community to attend or participate in the event.

In Honor of . . .

Students select someone from the community who has become famous—either at home or in the larger world. They can choose to read about the person or ask a knowledgeable person for information on what made him or her stand out from the crowd. Then help students write a poem about the accomplishments of the famous person. Some may easily choose a poetic form; others may need help. Give them a structure to begin, such as

"(Name of person) stands like a tree in our town."

Then students write ways in which the description of a tree might be used for the strength or beauty of the community figure.

You're Invited

Students write a letter to an organization they know about, inviting it to hold its next gathering in the community. It can be a sports organization such as a soccer league or an entertainment event such as the Country Music Awards ceremony.

The letter can be serious, taking into account the size and limitations of space. Or it can be humorous. For instance, you request to hold the World Olympics in a small town where the athletes stay in people's homes and practice in their backyards. Review the correct letter form, although students do not have to use real addresses.

Destination: Tokyo

With what students have read about a faraway community like Tokyo, have them think about how to start a pen pal letter with someone from a culture very different from their own. Some questions they may think of asking are:

- What are some things you do for fun in your community?

- What kind of clothes do you wear after school?

- What kind of music do you listen to?

Then ask students to make another list of their own interests or local surroundings that they might talk about in their letter. Have students start the letter with a brief introduction of themselves and then ask their questions. Remind them that this is only a *start* of a letter to practice setting up a friendly tone with someone they do not know.

Citizenship

Responsibility

**Things that sound too good to be true are often exactly that: not true.
Sometimes people make claims about things or places that are
not always true. Part of being a responsible citizen is to tell the truth.**

Sometimes advertisers exaggerate the good qualities of a product so that people will buy something. They hope for a result that may be different from the one they get.

Help students create a classroom game called Community Advertising Responsibility. First, ask volunteers to write on index cards statements suggested by you and other students about the local community. The statements can be true, false, or outrageous; the statements can be ones students have heard or ones they make up. Weed out inappropriate cards, make a deck, and shuffle it.

To play the game: Group 1 chooses a card from the deck and decides if the statement is true, false, or outrageous. If Group 2 objects, Group 1 has to prove it is true, false, or outrageous. The group wins points by giving the statement the correct label and by showing what makes an advertising statement a responsible one. Or, everyone can just play it as a "no-win, no-lose" game, going around the class and asking questions about a responsible statement. The game is over when all the cards have been used up.

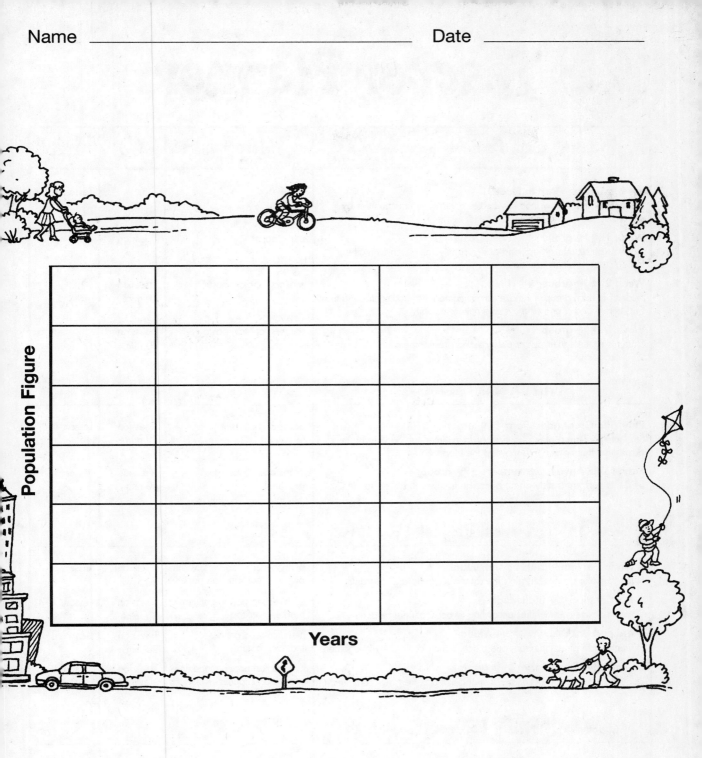

Population Figure

Years

Unit 2 Teacher Planner

Long-Term Project pages 26–27	Materials	🕐	Lesson Link
We Move From Place to Place Students examine how mobility creates diversity in communities by supposing they are a family.			Lesson 1
Week 1 👥👥 group Students break into groups and assign family roles such as mother, father, sister, brother, grandmother, etc.	pens, paper	1 session 20 min.	
Week 2 👥👥 group Students in each group will make posters comparing and contrasting their lives before and after their move to a new community.	scissors, photos, paste	1 session 30 min.	
Week 3 👥👥👥 group Students execute their poster designs and present them.	scissors, photos, paste	1 session 30 min.	

Unit Drama pages 28–33

	Materials	🕐	Lesson Link
Play: The Great Migration 👥👥👥 group Students perform a play about an African American Southern family deciding whether or not to move to the North.	props and costumes (optional)	1 session 30 min.	Lesson 1
Play: I Will Always Remember 👥👥👥 group Students perform a play about a foreign family emigrating to the U.S.	props and costumes (optional)	1 session 60 min.	Lesson 3

Chapter 3 Short-Term Projects pages 34–35

	Materials	🕐	Lesson Link
A Nation of Immigrants 👤 individual Students make graphs charting the ratio of citizens to immigrants.	pens, pencils, markers, white paper or construction paper	1 session 20 min.	Lessons 1–4
A Special Place 👤 individual Students devise communities according to occupational fields.	construction paper, pens or markers, oaktag	1 session 30 min.	Lessons 1–4
There and Back Again 👤 individual Students write directions from one place in their community to another.	pens, colored pencils, markers, oaktag	1 session 20 min.	Lessons 1–4
Community Vocabulary 👥👥👥 group Students list terms and definitions that originated in their own community.	construction paper, magazines, various art supplies	1 session 30 min.	Lesson 4

Chapter 3 Writing Projects pages 36–37

	Materials	🕐	Lesson Link
Wagons and Wings 👤 individual Students compare and contrast methods of travel over time.	paper, pencils	1 session 20 min.	Lesson 1
Who's Famous? 👤 individual Students make Famous Person Cards in order to learn more about important figures who either were born, or moved to their community.	paper, pencils	1 session 20 min.	Lessons 1–4
My Life and Times 👤 individual Students write journal entries from the point of view of a young person experiencing a new place.	paper, pencils	1 session 15 min.	Lessons 1–4

Social Studies Plus!

Chapter 3 Writing Projects *continued*	Materials	⏱	Lesson Link
Welcome to Your New Home 👥 **partners** Students write interviews by reporters from another community.	paper, pencils	1 session 25 min.	Lessons 1–4
Ten Little Words 👥 **partners** Students create a mini-glossary of words in foreign languages that may be spoken in their community.	paper, pencils, markers	1 session 20 min.	Lessons 1–4
Chapter 3 Citizenship Project page 38			
Fairness 👥👥 **whole class** Students make suggestions about fairness and bind into a book.	paper, pencils, index cards	1 session 45 min.	Lessons 1–4
Chapter 4 Short-Term Projects pages 40–41			
Let's Eat! 👤 **individual** Students draw place settings for federal or ethnic holidays.	construction paper, red clay, various art supplies	1 session 20 min.	Lesson 1
Meet Me at the Fair 👥 **partners** Students prepare brief reports about their community or county fair.	pens, colored pencils or markers, ruled & unruled paper	1 session 20 min.	Lessons 1–3
Beyond Tomorrow—Actually a Long Way Off 👤 **individual** Students create comic books about the building of their community.	watercolors, colored pencils or markers, construction paper	1 session 30 min.	Lessons 1–3
It's in the Kit 👤 **individual** Students design a "kit" of necessities for an ethnic celebration.	construction paper, oaktag, art supplies	1 session 30 min.	Lesson 3
Holiday Best 👤 **individual** Students create stick puppets dressed festively for a particular occasion, and see who can guess the holiday.	craft sticks, cotton, clay, glue, markers, paper, fabric supplies	1 session 30 min.	Lesson 3
Chapter 4 Writing Projects pages 42–43			
Would You Believe . . . ? 👤 **individual** Students write humorous fictional paragraphs about the day they won First Prize at the state fair.	paper, pencils	1 session 15 min.	Lessons 1–3
Where in the World? 👤 **individual** Students write poems about a holiday celebrated in a foreign country.	paper, pencils	1 session 25 min.	Lessons 1–3
In My Opinion . . . 👤 **individual** Students write letters to the editor of the community newspaper in support of a local celebration for someone.	paper, pencils	1 session 20 min.	Lessons 1–3
Compare and Contrast 👤 **individual** Students compare holidays in the United States with foreign holidays.	paper, pencils, reference material on foreign holidays	1 session 20 min.	Lesson 3
Chapter 4 Citizenship Project page 44			
Respect 👥👥 **whole class** Students examine different situations and decide whether they show respect or lack thereof.	pencils, BLM p. 45	1 session 45 min.	Lessons 1–3

NOTES

NOTES

Long-Term Project

We Move from Place to Place

Mobility creates diverse communities across the country. How do you think people from other places make a contribution to your community?

Getting the Idea

👪 group · ⏱ 20 minutes

Materials: pens, paper

The theme of this project is "We Move from Place to Place." Students will be making posters that illustrate this theme. Divide students into four groups. Each group will pretend to be a family.

• Group 1 has moved from another country to your community.

• Group 2 has moved from a different part of the country to your community.

• Group 3 has moved from a different kind of community to yours. (For example, if your community is urban, the group has moved from a rural or suburban community.)

• Group 4 has moved from one house to another within your community.

Students decide on the people who make up their family group. For example, if there are six in the group, there can be a mother, four children, and their grandfather or a mother and a father, two children, and their aunt and uncle. Students must also decide where they lived before. Group one may decide its family used to live in India. Group two may decide its family used to live in Seattle. Group three may decide its family used to live on a farm. Group four must decide on a specific part of their community where its family used to live.

Dividing the Tasks

♦♦♦ group   🕐 30 minutes

Materials: scissors, photos, and paste

The students in each group will make a series of posters that compare and contrast their lives before and after they moved to the new community. Here are some poster categories from which students may choose. Each student in a group is responsible for only one category.

- types of houses—old and new
- schools that the family children attend
- kinds of entertainment available
- foods and food shopping
- clothing (except for moves across town)

- the old and new neighborhoods
- jobs that family members hold
- celebrations
- community groups to join
- medical care available

Students decide which member of their "family" will cover each topic. For example, one of the "children" in the family will do the poster about schools. One of the "adults" in the family will do the poster about jobs. Celebrations and clothing can be from the point of view of either an adult or a child in the family.

The posters can have two columns or just two different areas depending on the amount of information. Heads for each column or area are:

In Our Old Home . . . In Our New Home

Students will gather research material for their posters. They should obtain between one and four pieces of information to compare and contrast. They should also gather photos to cut out and paste onto the posters or to copy for hand-drawn illustrations. Remind students to try to find equal amounts of items for both *before* and *after* parts of their posters.

Designing the Posters

♦♦♦ group   🕐 30 minutes

Materials: scissors, photos, and paste

Students plan the designs of their posters. They make their drawings or paste their photos and write short captions to go with them. When the posters are finished, the group makes a sign that tells where its family used to live. Each group makes a presentation to the class.

The Great Migration

In the early twentieth century, many African Americans moved from the rural South to cities in the North. This became known as the Great Migration. In this play a Southern family decides whether or not to move. Stage this play and think about how current events affected one family.

The Parts: (4 players)
- Mama
- Abe
- Papa
- Mabel, Abe's cousin

Director's Notes The stage should be divided in two. Abe and his parents pantomime eating dinner on one side of the stage. Cousin Mabel stands on the other side of the stage. She turns to face the audience when she has her first lines.

Mama: Abe, pass your papa the greens. *(Abe passes the greens.)*

Papa: I picked up this letter for you in town today.

Abe: *(excited, opening the letter)* Thanks, Papa. It's from Cousin Mabel.

Mama: Abe, you know there's no reading at the table. Your papa likes us to talk at supper. Isn't that right, dear? Dear? Is something wrong? *(Papa doesn't answer.)* Abe, go ahead and read your letter.

Abe: Thanks, Mama! *(reading aloud)* November 3, 1915. *(Abe now reads to himself. Cousin Mabel faces the audience and speaks.)*

Mabel: Dear Cousin Abe, how are you and Aunt and Uncle? How is the farm? Did your papa have a good cotton crop?

Mama: How much money did you get for the cotton?

Papa: After we pay the rent on the land and this house there's not much left.

Mabel: We are all fine here. We are having a party to celebrate moving.

Papa: What's that noise?

Mama:	Just this old house. The roof is leaking.
Mabel:	At the party, I'll eat ice cream and cake, potato salad, and fried chicken.
Mama:	Abe, would you like another piece of chicken?
Abe:	No thank you, Mama. Papa can have it.
Papa:	Skinny boys shouldn't give away food. Eat your chicken son.
Abe:	Yes, Papa.
Mabel:	Abe, I wish you could come to our party.
Mama:	What are we going to do?
Papa:	We'll borrow more money.
Mama:	It seems like we'll always owe someone money.
Papa:	We will if we stay here.
Mabel:	Papa says Chicago is a good place for us. We have good schools, good jobs, and our own newspaper. Papa and Mama read it every day. It's filled with news about the election.
Mama:	The North just seems so far away.
Mabel:	Papa and Mama are going to vote! Here in Chicago, no one will try to stop them. Mama says the best thing about the North is that we don't have to be afraid. We can live, and work, and even vote. Mama calls Chicago the Promised Land.
Mama:	I wish I knew what we should do.
Mabel:	Abe, there's one problem with Chicago. I miss you.
Papa:	Abe, your mama doesn't know if we should move North. What do you think?
Abe:	Cousin Mabel says Chicago is nice. They have good schools and lots of jobs. Chicago even has a newspaper for our people. Aunt and Uncle are going to vote next week.
Mama:	Vote? Let me see that letter. *(Mama and Papa look at the letter.)*
Papa:	Looks like Chicago has schools, jobs, opportunity. What do you think Mama?
Mama:	I think Abe better get ready for bed. It's a long trip North.

Chicago: North

I Will Always Remember

Can you remember as far back as the age of three? If you were separated from your father at that age, would you remember him five years later?

The Parts:	(6 players)
	• Two Narrators • Josep
	• Papa • Adolf
	• Mama

Director's Notes Place the family on one side of the stage. When Papa goes to the United States he can move to the other side of the stage. When the family joins him in the United States, they can meet center stage. Keep the Narrators in a place where they can be seen. Do not block the other actors. The old Polish folk song can be sung to the tune of "London Bridge Is Falling Down."

Narrator 1: The early twentieth century was a time when people from many parts of the world came to live in the United States.

Narrator 2: Sometimes one person from the family left first.

Mama: Do you have your ticket?

Papa: It's in my jacket pocket. *(Checking. Shows her ticket.)*

Mama: Oh, Janek, who will take care of you now?

Papa: Don't worry, Anna. It will only be for a short time.

Mama: I know. Come, boys, say good-bye to your papa.

Adolf: Good-bye, Papa. *(Papa and Adolf embrace.)*

Mama: Josep, say good-bye to Papa.

Josep: No. I won't! I won't! No. Don't go, Papa!

Adolf:	Baby, big baby.
Papa:	Adolf, Josep is only three. You are five. You must be kind to him. There, there, Josep, it's all right.
Mama:	Papa has to go. Don't you remember what I told you? There is opportunity in the United States.
Papa:	Don't worry. I'll send for you all very soon. Come let's sing our song. "Good luck, good cheer . . ." Come, Adolf, come, Josep. Sing with me and Mama. *(All sing.)*
All:	"Good luck. Good cheer. May you live a hundred years. Good luck. Good cheer. May you live a hundred years. One hundred years."
Papa:	Good-bye. I'll write.
All:	Good-bye, Papa, good-bye! Good-bye!
Narrator 2:	For a long time there was no letter from Papa and they were sad.
Narrator 1:	Finally, something came.
Mama:	Boys, I have a letter from your papa.
Josep and Adolf:	Yea, yea!
Mama:	My Dear Family . . .
Papa:	I hope this letter finds you all well. I am fine. I am working very hard. I will send for you soon. Don't worry. I am sure this year we will break the Christmas wafer together.
Josep:	Mama, how long until Christmas?
Mama:	Not long. Before you know it we'll all be together again.
Narrator 1:	But Christmas came and went.
Narrator 2:	Still the family was not together.
Mama:	*(reading from a letter)* My Dearest Family . . .
Papa:	I have a new job and I am saving money. It cannot be much longer before I am able to send for you. Surely we will eat mushroom soup and fried fish together this Easter.

Narrator 1:	Like Christmas, Easter came and went.
Narrator 2:	The boys were getting bigger and bigger.
Narrator 1:	They tried to be good but it was hard. They missed their papa.

(Adolf pinches Josep.)

Josep:	Ouch! If Papa were here you wouldn't get away with this.
Adolf:	Well, he's not here.
Josep:	When we go to the United States I'm going to tell him.
Adolf:	You don't even remember him.
Josep:	I do. I do remember.
Adolf:	Tell me one thing you remember. One thing he did or said.
Josep:	*(trying to remember)* He did . . . He said . . .
Adolf:	See, you don't remember.

Mama:	Boys! Sit down and listen. I have a letter from your papa. My Dear Family . . .
Papa:	I take up my pen to send good news. I have worked very hard and saved money to open a store. I sell meats and vegetables and many other things. There is a small home over my store. I am now ready for you to join me.
Narrator 2:	The trip was not easy. The family traveled by ship across the Atlantic Ocean.
Narrator 2:	Finally the ship sailed into New York Harbor.
Josep:	Look, Mama, look at the big green lady!
Mama:	That is the Statue of Liberty. She welcomes all newcomers to the United States.
Adolf:	When will we see Papa? I can't wait to see him.
Mama:	Soon, Adolf. We'll all be glad to see Papa.

Narrator 1:	But Josep was worried. Adolf was right. Josep couldn't remember his papa.
Narrator 2:	How would he feel meeting Papa again?
Narrator 1:	The ship docked and the Pulaski family went ashore.
Papa:	Anna, Adolf, Josep!
Mama:	Janek!
Adolf:	Papa, Papa!
Narrator 2:	Everyone rushed to hug Papa.
Narrator 1:	Everyone but Josep.
Papa:	Josep, is that you? You have gotten so big.
Mama:	Come and hug your papa.
Adolf:	He doesn't remember Papa.
Papa:	He's just feeling shy. Come, let's walk.
	(Papa hums a familiar tune . . . Josep stops in his tracks.)
Josep:	Papa! *(Sings.)* "Good luck. Good cheer. May you live a hundred years."
Papa:	That's right.
Papa and Josep:	*(singing)* "Good luck. Good cheer. May you live a hundred years. One hundred years."
Papa:	You remember our song?
Josep:	Yes, Papa. I remember you used to sing it to us. I remember! I remember!

Short-Term Projects

Communities across the United States develop their interesting flavor from longtime residents, people from other parts of the country, and recent immigrants. Read on for some projects in which students can begin to participate in the new community spirit.

A Nation of Immigrants

👤 individual   🕐 20 minutes

Materials: pens, pencils, or markers; plain white or construction paper

Every ten years there is a census in the United States. Explain to students that while a census counts the number of people living here, it also counts how many people came from foreign countries. During the years from 1900 to 2000, the number of foreign-born persons changed a great deal. Ask students why they think this happened. The figures on the right show for every hundred people in the United States how many were born elsewhere. Provide this information to the students so that each may make a line or a bar graph. Then have students illustrate the borders of their graph papers with their own impressions of a "nation of immigrants."

Year	Number
1900	14
1910	15
1920	13
1930	12
1940	9
1950	7
1960	5
1970	5
1980	6
1990	8
2000	10

Community Vocabulary

👥👥 group   🕐 30 minutes

Materials: colored pencils, pens, or markers; magazines; scissors; paste; construction paper

Many communities have their own slang, idioms, and special names for places, events, food, and other community favorites. For example: Pioneer Day honors the arrival of settlers in Salt Lake City, and hoagie is Philadelphia's name for a hero sandwich. Organize students to work in groups of three or four. Have each group put together a list of at least half a dozen such terms from their own community. Help them make a guide sheet listing the terms and short definitions, and find or make photos or illustrations for each term.

A Special Place

Materials: pens or markers; construction paper, oaktag, or cardboard

Communities are often organized according to common interests. Have students devise some communities according to common trades, for example, the medical "neighborhood," the entertainment "neighborhood," the bakery "neighborhood," and the musicians "neighborhood." Brainstorm other professions with students and write them on the board.

Then have students design street signs, lamp posts, traffic lights, telephone booths, or other common street fixtures that reflect the trade of the neighborhood. Street signs in "Medical Town" might have thermometers and stethoscopes. A telephone booth in "Music Town" might be in the shape of a saxophone. The design should incorporate colors, patterns, or symbols associated with the trade.

There and Back Again

Materials: pens, colored pencils, or markers; oaktag or cardboard

Remind students that for new people in a community, getting around can be a difficult experience. For people who don't know the language, it can be even more difficult. Have students select two well-known locations in the community. Ask them to write out directions from one place to the other. Then have students rewrite the directions using symbols whenever possible. For instance, use a left-turn sign, a bridge, or a railroad crossing to indicate directions.

Remember! Keep working on that Long-Term Project.

Writing Projects

Reading and writing about travel to new places is always exciting and helps your students examine their thoughts on the strange and the familiar.

Wagons and Wings

How did the first settlers arrive in your community? If it was an Atlantic coast community in the 1600s, it was probably by ship. If it was a newly-built Sunbelt community in the 1960s, it was probably by car, railroad, or plane. Discuss how travel has changed over time. Then have your students write paragraphs that compare and contrast the travel experiences from the past to those of the present. They should include the types of vehicles (and animals) used, how long the trips took, how hard they were, and what people might have brought with them from their former homes.

Who's Famous?

Provide students with a list of famous people who were born in your community or who have moved there. The people can be known in the community or in the larger world. Some research may be required. Have each student select one person and make a Famous Person Card on a 4-by-6-inch lined index card. Cards should provide the following information:

Name

Year of Birth (and Death)

Birthplace

Where Living When Famous

Claim to Fame

Ask each student to find or draw a picture of the famous person to place on the unlined side of the card. Gather all the students' Famous Person Cards and make a classroom collection of them. Encourage students to visit the collection and become familiar with the cards. You can feature one person a day during a Famous Person's Month.

My Life and Times

Lead the class in a discussion about times when new settlers in a community began to arrive. Then have students choose a period in history when newcomers were arriving in the community. The timeframe can be as recent as yesterday or as long ago as the first settlers, including Native American tribes. Each student creates a fictitious eight- or nine-year-old boy or girl and writes two journal entries that tell about the trip to the new community or the experiences of settling. Have students date their entries. At least one entry should contain something about an article of clothing, a vehicle, food, and a family member or friend.

Welcome to Your New Home

Lead students in a discussion about what it feels like to be a newcomer in a new place. Make a list on the board of possible newcomer reactions for students to consider. Then have students form pairs to write up an interview between someone who has recently moved to the community and a reporter for a newspaper, radio, or television show. The interviewee can be someone from another part of the United States or another country. The students can help each other write the parts. The student playing the reporter should ask questions that allow the student playing the new community member to explain why he or she has moved to the new place. There should be at least five questions and answers in the written interview. Students practice their interviews, then read them in front of the class.

Ten Little Words

What languages besides English are spoken in your community? Provide students with a list of languages. If you live in a small community there will probably be fewer languages spoken there than in a large city. Have students work in pairs. They should choose a language that isn't spoken at home. Ask pairs to make a list of ten words they would like to say in the other language. You and the students can research how to say the words in the other language. Then have them create a mini-glossary (in alphabetical order) with the English word, the word in the foreign language, and an illustration of the word. See the blackline master on page 39 for a format students can follow.

Citizenship

Fairness

Anybody who spends time around kids will eventually hear someone say "That's not fair!" Talking about what is and isn't fair can be a first step to finding workable solutions.

Create a class "Fairness" book. Write on the board: "It's not fair that . . ."; "It's not fair when . . ."; and "This can be made fair by . . ." Ask students to choose situations they think are unfair and write them on index cards or on small sheets of paper. On the backs of the cards or sheets of paper, have them write how they could make the situations fair. Students can submit as many situations as they wish.

Gather all the student writings and bind them into a book. Duplicate entries are fine because students may have different solutions. It will also show students that their classmates think some of the same things are unfair. You can organize the book around different themes, such as School, Home, Playground, Friends, and so on.

You may want to have a class Fairness Day in which you discuss student entries and suggest that students try to think about what it means to treat others fairly.

FAIRNESS

It's not fair that...

It's not fair when...

This can be made fair by...

Ten Little Words

English Word	Language	Drawing
_____	_____	_____
_____	_____	_____
_____	_____	_____
_____	_____	_____
_____	_____	_____
_____	_____	_____
_____	_____	_____
_____	_____	_____
_____	_____	_____

Short-Term Projects

Community celebrations are fun! Some celebrations have been around a long time. Others are newer since people bring them from faraway lands. As people exchange customs, their own experiences are enriched.

Let's Eat!

♦ individual   🕐 20 minutes

Materials: pens, colored pencils, or markers; construction paper, oaktag, or cardboard; red clay

Think of a celebration in your community for which you might have breakfast, lunch, dinner—or tea. Have students draw place settings for celebration meals. For example, for a meal celebrating the Fourth of July, they might draw red, white, and blue plates, red cups, white napkins, blue utensils, and a U.S. flag sticking out of a ball of red clay. For an ethnic celebration such as St. Patrick's Day, a color scheme of green and white with shamrocks might be used for decoration.

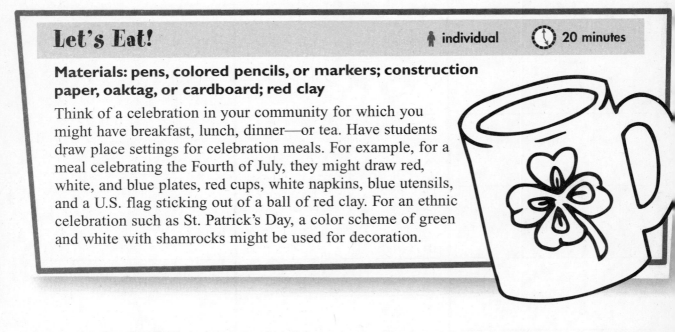

It's in the Kit

♦ individual   🕐 30 minutes

Materials: pens, colored pencils, or markers; construction paper, oaktag, or cardboard

Have each student design a "kit" that includes not only the place setting for the holiday but other things necessary for celebration. For example, the Fourth of July kit might include an outdoor grill, hot dogs, snacks, drinks, a flag, a picnic blanket, and bathing suits. The St. Patrick's Day kit might include the ingredients for Irish stew and soda bread, green lemonade, a leprechaun costume, and music for Irish songs.

Students don't actually make any of the items, but they have to determine how large their kits should be to fit everything. They may need to draw all the items and the box to check what fits. Perhaps they have so much stuff that they have to pack it in several boxes. Students need not confine themselves to the practical—tell them they can let their creativity run wild.

Holiday Best

👤 individual   🕐 30 minutes

Materials: craft sticks, cotton, clay, markers, bits of cloth and paper, buttons, sequins, ribbons, glue

Have students each choose a holiday in their community. Then have them decide on costumes that people might wear to celebrations on those holidays. Next, invite each student to make a stick puppet out of a craft stick, with cotton or modeling clay for a head (and body) and cloth or paper for clothes. The figure can be decorated with designs appropriate to the holiday. Have each student present his or her stick puppet to the class. The rest of the class has to guess for which holiday the puppet is dressed.

Meet Me at the Fair

👥 partners   🕐 20 minutes

Materials: pens, colored pencils or markers, lined and unlined paper

Find out where a state or county fair is held near your community. Provide students with a list of fairs or have students research what kinds of displays might be featured—what the star attractions are. Have each pair of students prepare a brief report about the fair and make illustrations of the attraction.

Remember! Keep working on that Long-Term Project.

Beyond Tomorrow–Actually a Long Way Off

👤 individual   🕐 30 minutes

Materials: watercolors, colored pencils, or markers; construction paper

Have students create comic books about the building of their community. Challenge them to show the different phases that the land went through. They may want to research which buildings or neighborhoods were built first and which more recently. Invite them to show future changes that could occur in their community. Encourage students to be creative.

Writing Projects

**Students research holidays and write newspaper op-ed articles
in some of these fun exercises.**

Compare and Contrast

Ask each student to compare a holiday that takes place in the United States with
one in another country. As they compare and contrast holidays, students should
focus on the following: Who celebrates the holidays? When do they take place?
What types of events usually mark the celebrations? What are the special foods,
costumes, and other customs? Students should organize their writing so that there is
a beginning (introduction), a middle (explanations of similarities and differences),
and an end (conclusion).

Would You Believe . . . ?

Ask students to write humorous fictional paragraphs
about the day they won First Prize at the
state fair. The prize can be for a very
large fruit or vegetable, an animal, or
arts and crafts. Include the following
information: What happened when the
judges saw it? How might students top
the entry next year?

Where in the World?

Have each student research a celebration that originated or is celebrated in a country other than his or her own and write a short poem about it. It could be a holiday such as N'cwala, which appears in the textbook, Carnaval (Rio de Janeiro), Bastille Day (France), Ramadan, St. Lucia's Day (Sweden), Hanukkah (Israel), Tet (Vietnam), Chinese New Year, Cinco de Mayo (Mexico). Explain to students that the poem can take a specialized form such as a haiku (three lines of five, seven, and five syllables), a cinquain (five lines), or an acrostic (where the first letter of each line spells out the name of the holiday). It can be in free verse, also. Tell students not to use the name of the holiday in the body of the poem. Finally, they read their poems to the class. Students have to guess what holiday is the poem's subject.

French Flag   Swedish Flag   Mexican Flag

In My Opinion . . .

Many newspapers have letters to the editor pages in which citizens can write in and give their opinions on a variety of subjects. Have each student prepare a letter to the editor for a community newspaper, urging that a local celebration be established for a person of his or her choosing. It can be a local or national celebrity, a government leader, or an all-around good person. Each writer should include what kinds of events should mark the day.

Citizenship

Respect

A well-known expression is "I get no respect." In real life, a lack of respect is no laughing matter. Do your students know what it is to be respectful? Do they know what it feels like not to be respected? The following exercise will make them think about the meaning of respect.

After conducting a discussion about respect, tell students they will play a class game called Respect. First, make up cards by photocopying, cutting up, and gluing onto card stock the squares shown on the blackline master on page 45, as well as any you wish to add. Have students draw one card at a time and tell if the situation shows respect or lack of respect. If the situation shows respect, the students explain what makes it that way. If it doesn't, then students tell why and how they could fix it.

The situations can be discussed with students before and after the exercise.

Respect

You work in your father's store. A woman and her daughter come in. They are dressed as if they have just arrived from Central America. They don't speak any English. You say, "Come back when you learn English."

One day you can't fit all your things into your locker. You see some space in an open locker that belongs to the new kid from France. You ask the French student if it's okay to use the extra space.

You are in the school lunchroom. A new student from Russia opens up her lunch bag. You close your eyes and hold your nose to show that her lunch is odd because it is different from yours.

Your friend's parents show you his baby pictures from when the family lived in Egypt. You are polite to them. But when you and your friend are outside, you complain how boring they are.

You're walking down the street. An old woman, leaning on a cane, asks you to stop. She shows you a piece of paper with an address on it. She asks how to get there. You walk with her to the address.

In gym class, a new student from Brazil can't climb the rope. All the other students in the class are impatient. Later, you tell the student that you will help her practice.

You are new in school. You miss your school and friends in Greece. You don't talk to anybody, even though you speak English. You tell your new teacher that you liked your teacher in Greece better.

Your new next-door neighbors are giving a party outside. Their music is loud and you can't sleep. You call the police.

One day your teacher is out sick. The teacher taking his place has an Australian accent. You make fun of his accent to make the rest of the students laugh.

Long-Term Project pages 48–49	Materials	🕐	Lesson Link
Where Are Communities? Students explore different physical environments of the world and create an exposition.			Lessons 1–3
Week 1 👥 whole class Students brainstorm different physical environments and record their ideas.	paper, pencils	1 session 30 min.	
Week 2 👥 group Students choose one physical environment to cover in an Environmental Expo booth.	paper, pencils, reference books	1 session 30 min.	
Week 3 👥 group Students select three distinct elements to include in their displays (for example, chart, model, and fact sheet).	picture books, various art supplies	1 session 30 min.	
Week 4 👥 group Students continue making displays, adding a colorful sign including the group's chosen region.	unfinished booth displays, picture books, art supplies	1 session 30 min.	
Week 5 👥 group Students take turns participating in the Environmental Expo tour, answering questions from their booth.	finished booth displays, classroom Expo area	1 session 30 min.	
Unit Drama pages 50–55			
Scenarios: Let's Improvise! 👥 group Students role-play skits about holidays and the Gold Rush.	index cards, pencils	2 sessions 20 min. each	Lessons 1–3
Play: A Town Council Meeting 👥 group Students perform a play about a town council meeting regarding environmental issues in the community.	props and costumes (optional)	1 session 30 min.	Lesson 1
Play: Learning the Rules 👥 group Students perform a play about Jane Addams' Hull House, and the immigrant experience.	props and costumes (optional)	1 session 30 min.	Lesson 1
Chapter 5 Short-Term Projects pages 56–57			
Hot or Cold Place Mat 👥 group Students design place mats showing people wearing appropriate clothing for a particular time of year.	thin cardboard, plastic wrap, crayons, markers, scissors, tape	1 session 20 min.	Lesson 2
Flap Fact Picture 👥 group Students create pictures of different physical environments throughout the world.	reference books, butcher paper, various art supplies	1 session 30 min.	Lesson 3

Chapter 5 Short-Term Projects *continued*	Materials	🕐	Lesson Link
Lovely Landforms 👤 **individual** Students make clay models of landforms they find fascinating.	clay, cardboard, picture books, construction paper, tape, scissors	1 session 15 min.	Lesson 3
A Mountain of Matches 👥 **partners** Students try to find a relationship between two cards with words written on them.	BLM p. 61, paper, scissors, pencils	1 session 20 min.	Lesson 3
Chapter 5 **Writing Projects** pages 58–59			
Weather Myth 👤 **individual** Students write humorous weather myths based on fantastic weather conditions.	paper, pencils	1 session 20 min.	Lesson 2
Vacation Here! 👤 **individual** Students write travel articles for their local newspaper.	paper, pencils, travel articles for reference	1 session 30 min.	Lesson 2
Weather Pros and Cons 👥 **partners** Students create pros and cons for various types of weather.	paper, pencils	1 session 15 min.	Lesson 2
Wild Weather Facts 👤 **individual** Students research fascinating weather facts in almanacs and write stories about them.	paper, pencils	1 session 20 min.	Lesson 2
Postcards Home 👤 **individual** Students write postcards home from their new community.	paper, pencils	1 session 25 min.	Lessons 1–3
Chapter 5 **Citizenship Project** page 60			
Responsibility 👤 **individual** Students examine different situations and decide whether they show responsibility or irresponsibility.	paper, pencils, index cards	1 session 45 min.	Lessons 1–3
Chapter 6 **Short-Term Projects** pages 62–63			
My Community Map 👤 **individual** Students make maps that show the community's location as a mountain, water, or crossroads type of community.	paper, markers*, community maps (optional)	1 session 30 min.	Lessons 1–3
Come to Seattle! 👤 **individual** Students choose one interesting Seattle site and create a colorful poster about it.	oaktag, markers, crayons, reference books	1 session 20 min.	Lesson 2
Fanciful House 👤 **individual** Students design houses for a mountain or waterside community.	paper, markers*	1 session 20 min.	Lesson 3
Climates of the World 👤 **individual/partners** 👥 Students label different regions of the world in a few descriptive sentences.	BLM p. 67, reference books, colored pencils	1 session 20 min.	Lesson 3

* or crayons

Teacher Planner

Chapter 6 Writing Projects pages 64–65	Materials	🕐	Lesson Link
Why is it There? 👤 individual Students research and write about a mountain range in the United States.	paper, pencils	1 session 20 min.	Lesson 1
Take Action! 👤 individual Students write a story about the courage they would need in order to take action to help others.	paper, pencils	1 session 20 min.	Lesson 2
A Daniel Boone Adventure! 👤 individual Students write journal entries from the perspective of a settler on an adventurous journey.	paper, pencils	1 session 20 min.	Lesson 3
Pioneer Fact-File 👥 partners Students research well-known pioneers and create a "fact-file" card about him or her.	paper, pencils, list of famous pioneers	1 session 20 min.	Lesson 3
Chapter 6 Citizenship Project page 66			
Courage 👥👥 whole class Students choose one courageous person and draw a four-to-six-panel cartoon showing the daily life of that person.	pencils, paper, markers*	1 session 40 min.	Lessons 1–3

* or crayons

NOTES

Long-Term Project

Where Are Communities?

**Where can you pick oranges or go fishing for crabs?
Where will you wear hiking shoes or rain boots? Explore the different
physical environments of the world and find out!**

Simulation: Environmental Exhibit

Week 1

👨‍👩‍👧‍👦 whole class 🕐 30 minutes

Materials: paper, pencils

Step 1. Tell your students that they are going to hold an Environmental Expo in the classroom. Remind them that a physical environment is made up of its landforms, climate, and resources.

Step 2. Ask children to list the kinds of food, clothing, buildings, and products that are found in each kind of physical environment. Help them to see how the natural resources of an environment affect what kind of businesses are located within them. Have children record and categorize their ideas. For example, the environment of Savannah, Georgia, might include warm-weather clothes, beach houses, crabs, shrimp, and people who fish for a living.

Plan an Expo Booth

Week 2

👨‍👩‍👧 group 🕐 30 minutes

Materials: paper, pencils, reference books

Divide the class into groups. Have each group choose one physical environment and its location. Make sure that each group chooses a different environment. Try to vary the locations chosen. Talk with children about how their ideas can be shown in a booth.

Have the groups make lists about how to decorate their booths, and what information and visuals to include in their booths. Children may decide to create a shoe box diorama showing the landforms and plants, along with handouts that tell how people have adapted to their physical environment.

Create Booth Displays

Week 3

👫👫 group   🕐 30 minutes

Materials: picture books, art supplies (shoe boxes, cardboard, juice boxes, clay, construction paper, oaktag, craft sticks), paper, pencils, glue, tape, scissors

Children may want to look at picture books to help them create displays. Guide the groups to include at least three different elements, such as a chart, a model, and a handout fact sheet. Show how to use modeling clay on a flat piece of cardboard to create a simple three-dimensional landform map. Guide your students to draw cartoons on their fact sheets to make them look more appealing.

Continue Making Booth Displays

Week 4

👫👫 group   🕐 30 minutes

Materials: unfinished booth displays, picture books, art supplies

Allow groups time to continue making their booth displays. Walk among the groups, offering suggestions. Ask: Will visitors to your booth want to visit the environment you have presented? Why or why not? What will visitors learn from your booth? Are you presenting information in a clear way? Have each group make a colorful sign for their booth. Guide them to include the name and type of their chosen physical environment.

Savannah Georgia

Southeastern Coastal region

Hold the Environmental Expo!

Week 5

👫👫 group   🕐 30 minutes

Materials: finished booth displays, classroom Expo area

Help students turn their classroom into the Environmental Expo. Use classroom desks and chairs to make "booths." Guide each group to display its booth's sign in a prominent place in or above the booth. Then have a volunteer from each group "host" the booth as others participate in a "tour" of the Expo.

Let's Improvise!

Improvise a situation! Get your creative juices flowing—and have some fun too!

Scenario 1: Pick a Holiday, Any Holiday!

Happy Thanksgiving! Trick or treat! Hooray for the red, white, and blue! Communities celebrate many different holidays. In this theater game students get to celebrate them all.

* First, have each student write the name of a holiday on an index card. It's fine if more than one student chooses the same holiday. However, it's best to get a good variety. Next, collect the index cards. Hold them fanned out like a deck of cards, the blank side facing students.

* Then, have students come up in groups of two to three. Each group selects a card. The students in the group then act out something associated with the holiday named on their card. The rest of the class must guess which holiday the group is acting out. For example, a group selecting Independence Day might sing patriotic songs while admiring the beautiful fireworks exploding above.

* Continue the game until every student has had a chance to play.

Scenario 2: The Rush Is On!

The Gold Rush brought people from all over the country to California in the late 1840s. In this exercise students imagine and act out what it was like to mine for gold.

- Brainstorm with students about what it was like to be in search of gold in the late nineteenth century. Tell them to suppose they are setting out in a Conestoga wagon for California and to think of some of the hardships that could happen along the way, such as hunger, thirst, surprise attack, heat, or sickness.

- Divide students into groups of five and have them decide among themselves why they are leaving their homes for California. Is it because they have been unable to farm in places like Oklahoma or Montana? Is it because they think they'll find enough gold so they'll never have to work again? Is it because they have heard that the climate in California is sunny and mild? Students can write their own reasons for taking part in the Gold Rush.

- They can also decide their relationships to each other within their group, for example, are they related family members or are they on their own? Encourage them to improvise scenes about why they are leaving for California. Invite them to perform their improvised skits in front of the class.

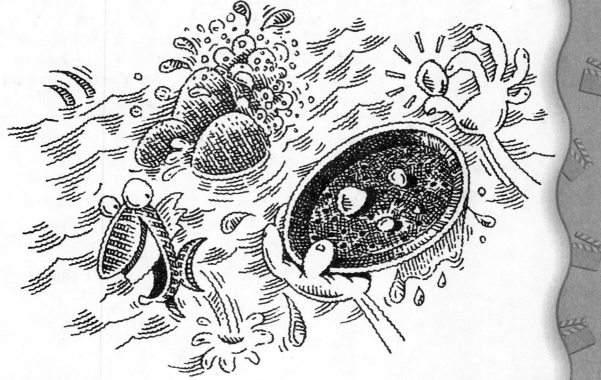

A Town Council Meeting

Town councils are one way that citizens get involved in their communities. Here's your chance to make changes!

The Parts: (6–8 players)
- 2 Speakers
- The Council President
- The Town Council (the audience)

Advance Preparation: *Explain that a business could be good for the community. However, the company wants to build its office on open land. There are many natural plants and wild animals on this land. There is a river with fish. Some citizens want the company to move to the community. Some citizens prefer that the land remain natural. Form two groups of two or three students each. One group will try to convince the council to let the company build in the community. The other group will try to convince the council to keep the land in its natural state. Tell each group to brainstorm at least three reasons to support its viewpoint. Before voting, the council must listen to both sides.*

 Director's Notes: Explain to your students that most of them will be playing members of the town council. Tell them their job is to listen carefully to both sides of the argument. They will then vote to decide whether they should allow a new company to move to their town. *Improv Directions* indicate where students make up their own dialogue.

President: I am the council president. My name is _____. Today we must make an important decision. Please listen to our speakers. They are representatives from the community and the business that would like to move here. Our speakers will now introduce themselves.

Speaker 1:   Thank you, Council President. My name is _____. I am a member of the Concerned Citizens. Thank you for inviting me here today.

Speaker 2: I would also like to thank the council for letting me speak here today. My name is _____. I work for the business that would like to move to this wonderful community.

President: Why are each of you here today?

Speaker 1: I want talk to you about preserving our natural environment.

Speaker 2: I want to speak to you about bringing our company to your community.

President: Please talk to us about your business.

Speaker 2: My business would be very good for the town. It would be good because _____.
(Improv Directions: Speak about your side of the issue.)

President: Thank you. May we now hear from our other speaker?

Speaker 1: A new business may bring some good things to our community. But I believe it will be bad for the natural environment. If we let this business move here this is what will happen: _____.
(Improv Directions: Speak about your side of the issue.)

President: Do any members of the Town Council have questions for our two speakers? *(Give members of the audience a chance to ask questions. Be sure that both speakers get equal time to respond.)*

President: Thank you both. Our council has a very hard decision to make. We will now vote. Those in favor of the new business, please raise your hands. *(Counts the votes.)* Those in favor of preserving the land, please raise your hands. *(Counts the votes.)* The council has decided that _____.

Thank you everyone.

Learning the Rules

Imagine what it would be like to move to a country where you didn't understand the language. How would you feel? What would you do?

The Parts: (3 players)
- Jane Addams
- Marco Santini
- Mrs. Santini, Marco's mother

Director's Notes: Remind your actors that Jane Addams started Hull House in Chicago in 1889. Hull House helped immigrants adjust to life in the United States. At the beginning of the play Jane is onstage alone, working at her desk. Opening and closing the door to Jane's office may be pantomimed. Have actors tap the floor with their feet to make the sound of knocking on the door.

Jane: *(Jane is at her desk in her office. There is a knock at the door.)* Come in.

Marco: *(entering)* Hello, Miss Addams.

Jane: Hello, Marco, how are you?

Marco: I am fine, Miss.

Jane: We missed you in art class today.

Marco: I'm sorry, I couldn't come.

Jane: Did you tell the teacher?

Marco: No, I didn't.

Jane: We have rules here. You must tell the teacher when you will miss class.

Marco: I'm sorry, Miss, I forgot.

Jane: The rules are written in every classroom. How could you forget?

Marco: I don't know, Miss. I just forgot.

CLASSROOM RULES

Jane:	Is something the matter, Marco?
Marco:	My mother is sick.
Jane:	What's wrong?
Marco:	She has a cough and a fever.
Jane:	Oh dear, has she seen a doctor?
Marco:	She is shy. My mother's English is not so good.
Jane:	We must go to her right away.
Marco:	She's outside.
Jane:	Well, bring her in. *(Marco gets his mother. Jane shakes her hand.)* Hello, Mrs. Santini. Welcome.
Mrs. Santini:	Hello, Miss Addams.
Jane:	You are not well? *(Mother does not understand. Jane points at Marco's mother and pretends to cough.)* You?
Mrs. Santini:	Yes.
Jane:	How long have you been sick? *(Marco's mother doesn't understand. Jane holds up a finger for each number she counts, still pretending to cough.)* One day? *(Coughs.)* Two days? *(Coughs.)* Three, four, five days?
Mrs. Santini:	*(holding up four fingers)* Four, four days. *(Coughs.)*
Jane:	Marco, tell your mother that we have a health clinic. She can see the doctor. *(Marco whispers to his mother.)*
Marco:	She will see the doctor.
Jane:	Good. Marco, did you miss class today because you were helping your mother?
Marco:	Yes, Miss.
Jane:	I see. Tell your mother we teach English here. Ask if she would like to learn. *(Marco whispers to his mother.)*
Mrs. Santini:	*(smiling)* Thank you, Miss. I want to learn English.
Jane:	Good. Take your mother to the doctor, Marco. *(They turn to leave. Jane calls out to them.)* Mrs. Santini, you must be proud of Marco. He is a very good boy. *(Marco smiles at Jane. He and his mother leave. Jane goes back to work.)*

Chapter 5

Short-Term Projects

Your students will have fun making place mats, posters, and more—as they explore physical environments and their effects on the people who call these environments home.

Hot or Cold Place Mat

👥 group   🕐 20 minutes

Materials: thin cardboard, plastic wrap, crayons, markers, scissors, tape

Divide your class into twelve groups. Have each group choose one month and design place mats for home or restaurant use that show people wearing appropriate clothing and doing appropriate activities for that month based on the average high temperature.

Encourage your students to be creative. For the place mats, have children cut out 12-by-8-inch rectangles from thin cardboard. Then have them write text and draw pictures on one side. When they finish, they can cover the illustrated side of the cardboard with plastic wrap and tape it onto the back. Voilà! A place mat!

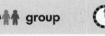

Flap Fact Picture

👥 group   🕐 30 minutes

Materials: reference books; butcher paper; scissors; tape; paints, markers, or crayons

Invite groups to make pictures of different physical environments throughout the world. Have each group leave space on their picture for labels that will tell important facts. Have groups list facts about how their physical environments influence the lives of communities, such as the foods that are eaten, clothing, types of buildings, and so forth. Each of these facts can be written on a label and taped onto the picture. The top edge of another label-sized piece of paper can be taped over each label to make a flap.

Have students decorate the flaps with colorful symbols or designs related to the facts beneath them. Hang the pictures side by side in a long row in order to compare the different physical environments. As students explore each other's pictures, they can lift the flaps to find the facts!

Lovely Landforms

👤 individual   🕐 15 minutes

Materials: clay, cardboard, picture books, construction paper, tape, scissors

Invite your students to make clay models of landforms they find particularly fascinating. Ask questions to get students thinking: Is there a lake or an ocean nearby where you have had fun? Have you ever picked wildflowers in a field or hunted for pinecones in a forest? Who has hiked a mountain?

1. Guide students to make their models on cardboard bases. Have them cut out labels from construction paper and write facts on them about the landforms.

2. Tell students to tape the labels onto their cardboard bases. Invite them to add personal notes along with their facts, such as "The Delaware River is a great place to go canoeing!"

Remember! Keep working on that Long-Term Project.

A Mountain of Matches

👥 partners   🕐 20 minutes

Materials: A Mountain of Matches Blackline Master (page 61), paper, scissors, pencils

Partners will enjoy playing this challenging matching game at their seats. Hand out a copy of A Mountain of Matches Blackline Master to each student. Have the students cut out each of the cards found on the page and mix them up. Cards should then be laid out facedown in a grid in order to play a matching game.

Players take turns choosing two cards and flipping them over. If the words on the cards can be related by the player, they are a match, and the player may keep the cards. For example, a player might relate the two words *river* and *fish* by saying, "A river is a landform where fish may live." If the player cannot relate the words, the cards are turned over again and play continues.

The game is over when all the cards have been matched. Students may want to create their own, similar cards from paper in order to keep playing the game.

Writing Projects

Chapter 5

Weather, weather all around! It affects our moods and our choice of clothes and activities. There's a story to be told for every kind of weather!

Weather Myth

How wet would you get if it rained for a hundred years? What if it got so windy that people could fly? Have children write humorous weather myths based on fantastic weather conditions. Encourage them to create heroes or heroines that can save people and animals from wild weather. Invite the children of your class to be as fanciful and descriptive as they like.

Children may wish to illustrate their weather myths and read them aloud to the class. Is it raining real raindrops, or are those *gumdrops?*

Vacation Here!

Tell your students they've just been hired to write travel articles for their local newspaper. Readers of the newspaper want to know the best time for vacationing in your community based on the weather.

1. Let students draw their own conclusions about which kind of weather and time of year is best suited for vacationers. Does your community feature mountain skiing? Then a snowy winter month will probably be the best time for that.

2. Guide students to include the answers to these questions in their articles: Who? What? Where? When? Why? How?

3. Model how to make the language of their articles lively and exciting. For example: "The best time of year to visit Smithtown is in January when our mountains are fluffy with snow. On a sunny day, the mountains sparkle like giant diamonds!"

4. Remind students to write headlines for their travel articles. Partners may wish to share articles and give suggestions for editing. Allow time for your "travel writers" to revise and polish their work.

Weather Pros and Cons

Have partners create a list of pros and cons for various types of weather. Guide them to choose a type of weather and then think of all the good things (the pros) and all the bad things (the cons) associated with it. For example, if the weather is warm and sunny, some pros might be "I can play outside. I don't have to wear a jacket." Some cons might be "I might get a sunburn. I will feel hot." Encourage students to compare and contrast their lists. Your class may want to take a vote based on the lists. Who likes snowy weather? Let's hear it for sunshine!

Wild Weather Facts

Have students research fascinating weather facts found in almanacs. Each should choose a specific fact, such as the height of a tidal wave, and include that fact in a story about wild weather. Students may wish to include more than one fact.

Guide students to try to write stories that could actually happen because of their weather facts. Model how to include dialogue to show how people in the story feel about the weather.

Postcards Home

Ask your students to write two or three postcards home from their new community. Give students a model: Someone who has just moved to San Francisco may write about what it is like to live near an ocean port. Before that person writes a postcard, to get started, he or she may think of questions such as, "Are there a lot of ships in the harbor that are coming and going? What cargo do the ships carry? Who works on the ships? Who travels on the ships? Is there a certain time of day when I can see the ships being unloaded? Do crews from fishing boats bring their catch to the port early in the morning?" Encourage students to make their postcards as vivid as possible. They may use reference books for ideas.

Chapter 5 Citizenship

Responsibility

Let's take care of ourselves and each other! It's a wonderful world when everyone acts responsibly!

Talk with your students about what it means to act responsibly. Give them this scenario: You have promised to help a family member clean the house, but your friend asks you to come over, and you want to play. What is the responsible thing to do? After students have given correct responses, ask them: What is the irresponsible thing to do? Make sure your students know the difference between responsible and irresponsible behavior.

With the class, brainstorm situations in which people will be given a choice whether to act responsibly or irresponsibly. For example: You borrow a friend's toys. You get a new puppy. You find someone's lost backpack. List students' responses on the chalkboard. Then have each student choose several items from the list and write each one on a separate index card.

Divide the students into groups. Divide up the index cards so that each group has the same amount. Have each group put its index cards into a paper bag. Then ask each group member to take a turn pulling a card out of the bag and reading the situation. That member must give an example of responsible and irresponsible behavior for that situation. For example, if the situation is "You get a new puppy," an example of responsible behavior might be "I will feed it and play with it." An example of irresponsible behavior might be "I will try to remember to feed the puppy, but if I forget, someone else will do it for me." Have each group member take at least one turn. If time allows, gather the class together and talk about how much better the world would be if everyone acted responsibly!

A Mountain of Matches

River

Fish

Mountains

Snow

Desert

Sun

Forest

Lumber

Ocean

Beach

Hills

Hiking

Short-Term Projects

Mountains, bodies of water, and the weather
that warms them up or cools them down—your class will get
a chance to explore these ideas through a variety of fun projects.

Fanciful House

👤 individual   🕐 20 minutes

Materials: paper, markers or crayons

Give your students an opportunity to design fanciful houses for a
mountain or waterside community. Encourage them to be
creative and to focus on the landform of the
community. People living in a mountain community,
for instance, might want to ride a cable car from the
bottom of the mountain up to their home. Perhaps their
house has a special platform above it for the cable car to
park when it drops them off. This platform may be
attached to a slide so the people can slide right down
into their front yard! Have students draw pictures of their
fanciful house designs. Then have each student write a few
sentences telling how the features of the house work with
the major landform of the community.

My Community Map

👤 individual   🕐 30 minutes

Materials: paper, crayons or markers, simple community maps (optional)

Ask your students to make maps that show their community's location as a mountain,
water, or crossroads type of community. Guide them to make simple maps, showing only
those features and locations that are necessary for someone
to understand which type of community the map shows.
If available, allow groups to look at simple community
maps to give them ideas and help them check the
locations of features and other important landmarks.

Suggest that students include compass roses and write
simple labels for their maps' features. Have them write
the name of their community on the maps and color
them attractively.

Map of Manhattan

Empire
State
Building

N
W   O   E
S

Climates of the World

Materials: Climates of the World Blackline Master (page 67), reference books, colored pencils

Some regions of the world are wet and warm, and others are so cold only a polar bear could survive! Hand out copies of the Climates of the World Blackline Master to the children in your class and have them color in the different regions.

Ask them to label each region with a few descriptive sentences or facts. For example, children may label the tundra region with this fact: "The ground is frozen about ten months of the year." Allow children to use reference books to help them research their facts. Partners may wish to take turns quizzing each other about the regions found on the climate maps.

Remember! Keep working on that Long-Term Project.

Come to Seattle!

👤 individual   🕐 20 minutes

Materials: oaktag, markers, crayons, reference books

From the sparkling waters of Elliot Bay and Puget Sound to the top of Mount Rainier—there's a lot to see in Seattle! Guide your students to each choose one interesting Seattle sight and create a colorful poster about it. Encourage students to look through reference picture books to get ideas and model how to look for interesting and important details in the pictures. For example, you may talk about how to show the scale of the three-mile-high Mount Rainier by showing some very tiny people at its foot. Students may wish to write lively slogans about the Seattle sights on their posters. For example: "Mount Rainier—we're glad it's here—in Seattle!" Hang students' work in a classroom display.

Mount Rainier- we're glad it's here- in Seattle!

Creativity is sparked as your students put pens to paper and write about mountain communities, Wilderness Trail journeys, extreme weather, and more!

Why Is It There?

Mountains may well be our world's most majestic kind of landform. Ask your students each to choose a mountain range inside the United States with which they are familiar or one they would like to know more about.

Have each student then choose and research information about a community found in or near this mountain range. Ask him or her to write about the community, and to draw conclusions about why it was founded in or near the mountain range.

Take Action!

Have children think about what it's like to be present during an extreme weather event in their community such as a tropical storm or a drought. Suggest that they write made-up stories describing the courage they would need in order to take action and responsibility to help others. For example, children might write about how they had to try to act bravely in order to help calm others who were scared. Maybe they invited friends whose homes were damaged to stay at their houses. Encourage children to add descriptive details about how the weather affected the physical look of their community. Ask: Were trees and power lines affected? Were roads flooded or blocked by debris?

A Daniel Boone Adventure!

What if Daniel Boone had asked your students to accompany him as he made the Wilderness Trail? Have each student write three or four short journal entries from the perspective of a settler on this adventurous journey. Guide your students to think of themselves as settlers, what they might have encountered in the mountains, and what it was like when they finally reached the Kentucky River area. Have them try to include sights, sounds, and smells in their journal entries to make their entries come alive. Ask: What was Daniel Boone like as a leader? Was he kind and fair? Was he brave? How did he make you feel? Who else was on the journey with you? What was your work like? Was it hard to make the trail?

Pioneer Fact-File

Provide children with a list of famous pioneers such as Daniel Boone, Annie Oakley, Davy Crockett, Johnny Appleseed, Calamity Jane, Buffalo Bill, and Kit Carson. Group the children in pairs and have each pair choose a different pioneer to research in order to create a "fact-file" card. To make the card, have them cut 5-by-5-inch squares of oaktag. On the front of the card, each child should make a drawing that represents his or her pioneer. The back of the card should list important information about the pioneer. When children complete their fact-file cards, they may help decorate a shoe box to make a fact-file card holder. Collect all the finished cards and put them in the card holder. Encourage children to refer to it in their future research.

Citizenship

Courage

**Who's the bravest of them all? What does a courageous person do all day?
Is that person like you and me?**

Tell your students that they are going to draw cartoons about the daily lives of courageous
people such as Harriet Tubman. Discuss with them how courageous people often risk their own
safety in order to help others. Brainstorm a list of courageous people found in your community,
such as firefighters, police officers, emergency room workers, and ambulance drivers. You may
also want to focus on what kind of courage it takes for immigrants to come to a new country.

Have students each choose one courageous person and draw a four-to-six-panel cartoon showing
the daily life of the person. Guide students to show the people in situations that portray their
courage and the risks they might have to take. Model how to write speech balloons for the
characters in the cartoons.

Students may want to do some prewriting before they draw the actual cartoons. They can first
sketch out ideas rather than making detailed drawings. If they see things they want to change,
they can make revisions without too much difficulty. Allow partners to give feedback on each
other's ideas. This will also help students when they want to create their final cartoons.

Encourage students to write lively text in their speech balloons and to make their cartoons fun
and colorful. Remind them that an act of courage is often a very exciting thing to see.

Have students share their cartoons with the rest of the class. Hang them in a classroom "Display
of Courage!"

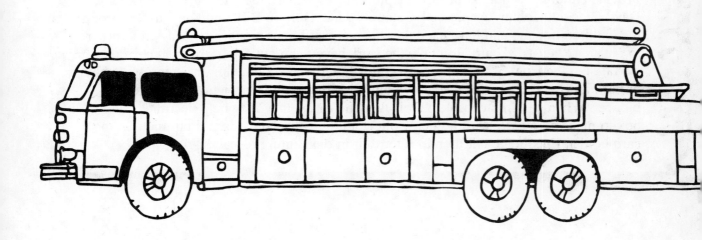

Climates of the World

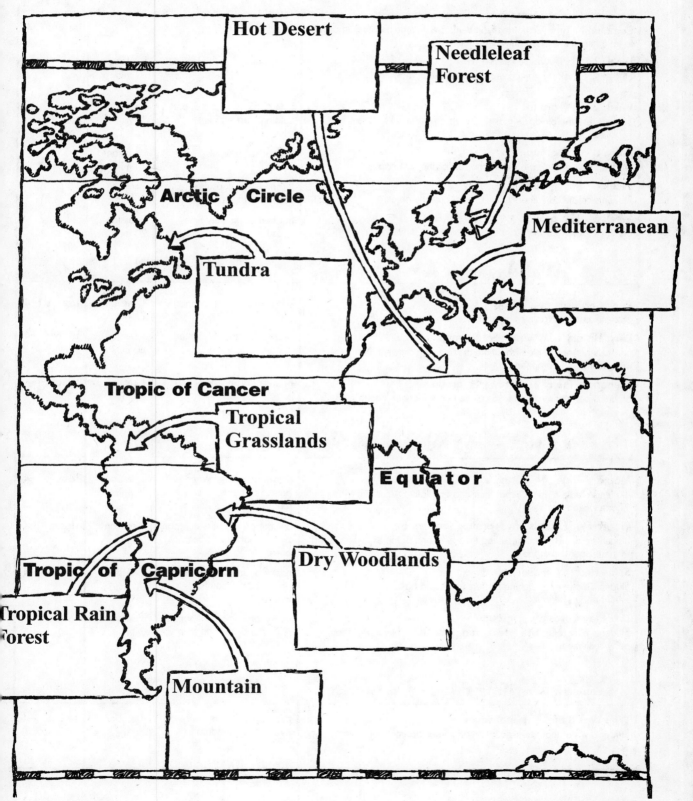

Unit 4 Teacher Planner

Long-Term Project pages 70–71	Materials	🕐	Lesson Link
Community Time Capsules! Students create time capsules in order to let others know about their community.			Lessons 1–4
Week 1 👫👫 **whole class** Students brainstorm objects and keepsakes that they would like to include in their time capsule.	pens, paper	1 session 30 min.	
Week 2 👫👫 **group** Students use the blackline master cutouts on page 83 for their time capsules.	BLM p. 83, magazines and catalogs, art supplies	1 session 30 min.	
Week 3 👫👫 **group** Students revise and polish their choices for the time capsule.	various art supplies	1 session 30 min.	
Week 4 👫👫 **group** Students create containers for their time capsule objects.	finished time capsule contents, art supplies	1 session 30 min.	
Week 5 👫👫 **group** Students search for and "dig up" other groups' time capsules.	finished community time capsules	1 session 20 min.	
Unit Drama pages 72–77			
Play: Because 👫👫 **group** Students perform a play about why certain things happen.	props, costumes (optional)	1 session 25 min.	Lessons 1–4
Play: History's Mysteries 👫👫 **group** Students perform a play about the first meeting between Native Americans and Europeans.	props, costumes (optional)	1 session 40 min.	Lessons 1–4
Scenarios: The Big Picture 👫👫 **group** Students pantomime what takes place in a variety of locations.	no materials needed	1 session 20 min.	Lessons 1–4
Chapter **7** **Short-Term Projects** pages 78–79			
Map a Village 👫 **partners** Students create maps of what their chosen Native American tribe's village looked like.	drawing paper, colored pencils or markers, simple maps	1 session 20 min.	Lessons 1–4
Picture-Story Bands 👫👫 **group/partners** 👫 Students make a frieze depicting the life of one of the explorers found in the textbook chapter.	butcher paper, scissors, tape, paints, markers*, reference books	1 session 30 min.	Lessons 1–4
Settle Here! 👤 **individual** Students make eye-catching posters that could have been used to attract early settlers.	poster board or drawing paper, poster paints, markers*	1 session 20 min.	Lessons 1–4
Let's Play Cards 👫👫 **group** Students play a Go Fish type of card game while they learn about early settlements.	index cards, markers, simple reference books and maps	1 session 30 min.	Lesson 4
Chapter **7** **Writing Projects** pages 80–81			
Why Was It Built? 👤 **individual** Students write about historic landmarks in or around their community.	paper, pencils, reference materials on landmarks	1 session 30 min.	Lessons 1–4

* or crayons

Chapter 7 Writing Projects *continued*	Materials	🕐	Lesson Link
A New Name 🛉 individual Students come up with a new name for their community and write about why their name will improve upon the old one.	paper, pencils	1 session 20 min.	Lessons 1–4
Explorer Acrostic Poem 🛉 individual Students write acrostic poems about an explorer they have read about.	paper, pencils	1 session 20 min.	Lessons 1–4
Bag of Riddles 🛉 individual Students write riddles about historic places in or around their community.	paper, pencils	1 session 30 min.	Lessons 1–4
Chapter 7 Citizenship Project page 82			
Caring 🛉🛉🛉 group Students create Caring Heart Pockets to present to other classes.	paper, pencils, oaktag, markers, hole punch	1 session 45 min.	Lessons 1–4
Chapter 8 Short-Term Projects pages 84–85			
Travel Time Line 🛉 individual Students create time lines about travel inventions.	reference books, old magazines or catalogs, art supplies	1 session 20 min.	Lesson 1
Travel by Train! 🛉🛉 partners Students write radio advertisements encouraging people to travel by train.	paper, pencils, audiocassette recorder (optional)	1 session 30 min.	Lesson 1
Important Invention Portraits 🛉 individual Students pay tribute to a favorite important invention.	photographs or other visual reference materials, art supplies	1 session 20 min.	Lessons 1–4
Morse Code Bracelets 🛉🛉 partners Students make message bracelets written in Morse code.	BLM p. 89, construction paper, scissors, markers, tape	1 session 20 min.	Lessons 1–4
Chapter 8 Writing Projects pages 86–87			
All Aboard! 🛉 individual Students write journal entries describing a trip they would like to take within the United States.	paper, pencils	1 session 20 min.	Lesson 1
Saddle Up! 🛉 individual Students write speeches persuading young men and women to become riders for the Pony Express.	paper, pencils	1 session 20 min.	Lesson 2
What If? 🛉 individual Students write descriptive letters to Thomas Edison thanking him for his inventions.	paper, pencils, reference materials on Edison's inventions	1 session 20 min.	Lesson 3
Inventive Inventor Poems 🛉🛉 partners Students write poems about a particular inventor.	paper, pencils	1 session 30 min.	Lessons 1–4
Invention Unscramble 🛉🛉 partners Students write inventions as scrambled words and see if a partner can unscramble them.	paper, pencils, reference materials on inventions from the 1940s	1 session 20 min.	Lessons 1–4
Respect 🛉🛉🛉🛉 whole class Students brainstorm several examples of situations where a person deserves respect.	pencils, construction paper, markers*	1 session 40 min.	Lessons 1–4

* or crayons

NOTES

NOTES

Long-Term Project

Community Time Capsules!

What would you put in a time capsule to let others know about life in your community? In one hundred years, community members can dig up the capsule and get a peek at their past!

Brainstorm About Time Capsules

Week 1

👨‍👩‍👧 whole class   🕐 30 minutes

Materials: paper, pencils

Time capsules are a great way to record history. Explain to your class that a time capsule is a container filled with objects, pictures, and other important keepsakes that help people in the future know what a place is like.

Brainstorm with students about the different things that could be included in a time capsule. Suggest that they think of things that tell people about present-day school, free time, food, music, clothes, communication, and other important customs or ideas. Record students' responses.

Create Capsule Contents

Week 2

👨‍👦 group   🕐 30 minutes

Materials: lists from Week 1, Community Time Capsules Blackline Master on page 83, scissors, colored pencils and markers, old magazines and catalogs, construction paper, glue

Divide the class into groups. Explain that each group will create its own unique time capsule. Tell students that instead of actual objects, they are going to use cutouts from the blackline master, magazines and catalogs. If convenient, use this procedure:

1. Hand out a copy of the blackline master, art supplies, and a piece of colored construction paper to each member of each group.

2. Each group chooses an area for its time capsule such as School or Transportation.

3. Students draw lines dividing their paper into four equal squares and glue one cutout into each square.

4. Students may write why their cutouts are important for people in the future to know about.

Week 3

Creating More Capsule Contents

👤👤 group   🕐 30 minutes

Materials: supplies from Week 2

Work with groups to make sure they have adequately covered their time capsule subjects. Ask students to check and see if they have repeated pictures or wish to make any changes. Allow time for groups to revise and refine their work.

Week 4

Making Time Capsules

👤👤 group   🕐 30 minutes

Materials: finished time capsule contents from Week 3, quart–sized plastic containers or shoe boxes, poster paints and paint brushes, tape

Step 1. Create a time capsule by taping the open ends of two quart-sized containers together or by using a shoe box and a lid. (Do not tape containers together before placing the time capsule contents inside!)

Step 2. Paint decorations on the time capsules.

Step 3. Label time capsules with the community name and the date.

Step 4. After the capsules are dry, fold the pages and place them inside the capsules.

Step 5. "Bury" the capsules somewhere in the classroom.

Week 5

Dig Up Time Capsules

👤👤 group   🕐 20 minutes

Materials: finished Community Time Capsules

Have groups search for and "dig up" other groups' time capsules. Then hold a mock ceremony that takes place one hundred years from now. Each group can then open another group's time capsule and examine it as if they were living in the future. What will they learn about the "old-fashioned" past?

COMMUNITY TIME CAPSULE

Because

Sometimes it's hard to explain why certain things happen. Does everything always happen for a reason? Stage this play to find out.

The Parts: (7 players)
- Narrator 1
- Narrator 2
- Five Friends (Mary, Jose, Sue, Carl, Bob)

 Director's Notes: In this play, some scenes are scripted. In other places, actors must *improvise*.

Narrator 1:	Everything happens for a reason. Everything has a cause and effect.
Narrator 2:	A cause is an action.
Narrator 1:	The effect is the result of an action.
Narrator 2:	In this play we'll improvise a cause and act out the effect.
Narrator 1:	Our story is about Bob and his friends.
Narrator 2:	Bob's friends are worried about him. He's been very sad lately.
Narrator 1:	Bob is the school's star basketball player.
Narrator 2:	Well, he was until he broke his leg last week.
Narrator 1:	Now he can't play ball or go to school for a while.
Narrator 2:	But his friends have a plan to cheer up Bob.
Narrator 1:	Here we go. The scene begins.
Mary:	We only have about ten minutes before Bob and his mother come home from the doctor's office.

Jose:	Then let's get to work.
	*(**Improv Directions:** Bob's friends put out food, hang balloons and streamers and set up a big trophy that says 'Most Valuable Player'. They talk as they mime these activities.)*
Sue:	Listen, I think they're here.
Carl:	Quick, let's hide.
Bob:	*(from offstage)* Mom, I'm going to watch TV in the family room. *(Bob enters. His friends jump out of their hiding places.)*
All:	Surprise! Surprise!!
Narrator 1:	Freeze! *(The actors freeze in place.)*
Narrator 2:	Let's review cause and effect.
Narrator 1:	A cause is an action.
Narrator 2:	The effect is the result of an action.
Narrator 1:	What action did Bob's friends take?
Narrator 2:	They gave him a surprise party.
Narrator 1:	Why did they give him a surprise party?
Narrator 2:	Because they wanted to cheer him up.
Narrator 1:	Let's see if it works.
Bob:	What are you guys doing here?
Jose:	We are having a party for you.
Sue:	Look, we got you a trophy.
Bob:	You guys are great.
Narrator 1:	Yes, everything happens for a reason. Friends can do things to cheer up friends who feel sad.
Narrator 2:	Our actions cause things to happen. That's what is known as cause and effect.

History's Mysteries

There are times in life when we see or learn something we could never have imagined. The play, "History's Mysteries," tells a story about the first meeting between Native Americans and Europeans.

The Parts: (6 players)
- Narrator 1
- Narrator 2
- Mother
- Gray Wolf
- Red Sun
- Father

🎥 **Director's Notes:** The narrators stand in the center of the stage. The boy and girl speak in front of, but not blocking, the narrators. The boy and girl run in one direction when they go to the water. They run in the opposite direction when they return home.

Narrator 1: History gives us stories of the past. We learn what happened, where, and when.

Narrator 2: So tell us, where are we?

Narrator 1: In the Americas. This land will one day become the United States.

Narrator 2: What time is it?

Narrator 1: It is a long time ago, over four hundred years in the past.

Narrator 2: Who lives here?

Narrator 1: Native Americans call this place home. They live in long wooden houses made from the bark of trees. The women tend the garden while the men hunt for food. And the children do what children have always done.

(A boy and girl enter laughing. They chase each other in a large circle around the narrators.)

Gray Wolf:	First one to the water wins.
Red Sun:	Catch me if you can!
Narrator 2:	Who are they?
Narrator 1:	Red Sun and her brother, Gray Wolf.
Red Sun:	I won! I won!
Gray Wolf:	I must have had a pebble in my moccasin.
Red Sun:	You always say that when I win.
Narrator 2:	They look like they're having fun.
Narrator 1:	Watch them carefully. They are about to make an important discovery.
Gray Wolf:	Red Sun, look at that.
Red Sun:	I don't see anything.
Gray Wolf:	Look, there where the water meets the sky.
Red Sun:	Is that a sea animal rising out of the water?
Gray Wolf:	I don't know.
Red Sun:	It moves so fast.
Gray Wolf:	It is moving in this direction.
Narrator 1:	Red Sun and Gray Wolf watched the strange sight for a long time.
	(Now Red Sun and Gray Wolf run in the opposite direction around the circle.)
Narrator 1:	Then they ran back home.
	(Their mother and father come over to them.)
Father:	Calm down, children.
Mother:	We cannot understand you when you speak so fast.
Father:	What is it you saw?
Gray Wolf:	We don't know.
Mother:	Where did you see this thing?

Red Sun:	We saw it on the water. It was so big.
Gray Wolf:	It looked like a long house.
Red Sun:	It looked like a long house turned upside down.
Gray Wolf:	From the top of the house were long poles.
Red Sun:	With big white clouds tied to the poles.
Gray Wolf:	Have you ever seen such a thing, Mother?
Mother:	No, I have not.
Red Sun:	What could it be, Father?
Father:	I do not know.
Mother:	Come, show us what you have seen.

(The family walks back around the circle to the water.)

Narrator 2:	It's only a ship.
Narrator 1:	But they have never seen anything like it.
Narrator 2:	The ship must be from Europe.
Narrator 1:	It will be the first of many to come.
Father:	We must tell the elders.
Mother:	Everyone must see this.
Narrator 2:	Think of all the things the Native Americans will learn from the Europeans.
Narrator 1:	And the many things the Europeans will learn from the Native Americans.
Red Sun:	What will happen?
Narrator 2:	Today we know what was in store for Red Sun, Gray Wolf, and their family. Back then it was all a mystery.
Mother:	Time will show us.
Narrator 1:	There is only one thing that any of us can know about the future. It always brings change.

The Big Picture

In this theater game, students pantomime
what takes place in a variety of locations.
As their classmates guess the location they join the fun.

The Big Picture

Students learned about the function of a locator map in this unit— that it shows where a place is in a larger area. This theater game uses an activity to locate or indicate the larger setting in which the activity takes place.

Here's how the game works. One or two students pantomime an activity to give the audience a clue about the setting. For instance, a student may mime rolling out dough, throwing it into the air, covering it with tomato sauce and cheese, then placing it in the oven to make pizza. This would locate the activity in a pizza parlor.

When an audience member recognizes the setting that person may join the improvisation. Other students can play customers, cashiers, delivery people, and so forth.

Students can think of their own settings, but here are some suggestions of settings for activities:

bowling alley
supermarket
gym
classroom
hospital
movie theater
playground
park
cafeteria
living room

Short-Term Projects

We'll explore early settlement communities in these fun
and easy projects. Who was living there? Who wanted to go? What did the
early communities look like? Students create maps, mobiles, picture-story bands,
colorful cards, and more to help them find out.

Map a Village!

👫 partners   🕐 20 minutes

Materials: drawing paper, colored pencils or markers, simple maps for reference

Ask your students to imagine what an early Native American village looked like.

• Where did the Native Americans put their homes?

• Where did they farm and hunt?

• Where did they hold their religious ceremonies?

Invite partners to choose a Native American tribe with which they are familiar or want to learn more about. Then have them create a simple map showing what they think their chosen tribe's village looked like. Provide students with simple maps showing map keys and symbols for features such as mountains, rivers, forests, farmlands, dwellings, and other important locations. Have partners include a compass rose and a map key for their features.

Settle Here!

🧍 individual   🕐 20 minutes

Materials: poster board or drawing paper; poster paints, markers or crayons

What's the best way to get people to move to a new place? Advertise! Have children create an eye-catching poster that could have been used to attract early settlers, highlighting one of the historic settlements, such as Jamestown, Quebec, or St. Augustine. Suggest that children think of all the positive things about the new community and why that place might appeal to new settlers. Remind children that many advertisements use colorful adjectives such as *amazing* or *sky blue*.

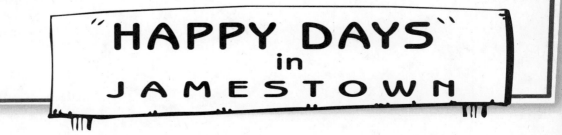
"HAPPY DAYS" in JAMESTOWN

Let's Play Cards!

Materials: index cards, markers, simple reference books and maps

Your students will have fun playing a Go Fish type of card game while they learn about early settlements.

1. Have each group choose an early settlement, such as Oneida County, Jamestown, Quebec, or St. Augustine.

2. Use simple reference books and maps to create playing cards with pictures about their chosen settlements. Some facts may include who discovered the land, where and when the settlement was built, and why.

3. Have each group make two sets of ten cards. Shuffle all the completed cards together.

4. Each group member is dealt a hand of five cards. The players then take turns asking each other for types of settlement cards in order to make matches.

Picture-Story Bands

Materials: butcher paper, scissors, tape, paints, markers or crayons, reference books (optional)

Invite students to make a frieze depicting the story of the life of Pocahantas, Sacagawea, or one of the explorers found in Chapter 7. Explain that a frieze is a band of pictures that tells a story and often decorates a wall. Groups or partners may work together to research ideas for their friezes. Tell them to make a list of the pictures they think would be important to include in their picture-story bands.

Guide groups to cut 4-by-24-inch pieces of butcher paper to make the bands on which to draw pictures from left to right to tell a story. Guide students to make their friezes colorful and clearly told. Display and talk about the friezes.

**Remember!
Keep working
on that
Long-Term Project.**

Writing Projects

Chapter 7

One community is worth ten thousand words—or more! Invite your students to write poems, acrostics, and other descriptive pieces on the fascinating subject of communities.

Why Was It Built?

Your community probably has a number of historic treasures such as landmarks and buildings that have been preserved from long ago. Provide children with a list of these historic treasures and some reference materials about them, if available. Then have children write a short piece about an historical landmark and explain:

- why it was built and by whom,

- if it's still being used and how,

- what steps have been taken to keep it maintained.

After the children finish writing, have them take a break and do something else before looking at their drafts again. Then ask them to read over their work to add or remove words to make the writing clearer and more interesting.

A New Name

What's so great about names? Plenty! A name can describe, honor, or invite curiosity about a place. Give students the opportunity to think up a new name for their community and write a short piece about why they think this new name will improve upon the old one.

Perhaps your class can vote for the best new name for your community. For example, would they like to honor an important community member by renaming the community after that person? Is there a popular flower or tree in your community? Encourage creativity!

Explorer Acrostic Poem

Acrostic poems are an unusual and interesting way to write about a subject. Show students how, in an acrostic poem, a word or name is written vertically. Explain that the first letters of this word or name are used to begin the lines of the poem. Often, these first letters are written bigger or more boldly than the other letters in the poem so that it is easy to see them. Invite students to write an acrostic poem using the name of one of the explorers they have read about. The lines of the poem can be a single word, a phrase, or a complete sentence. For example, if students choose Christopher Columbus, the first four lines of the poem might be:

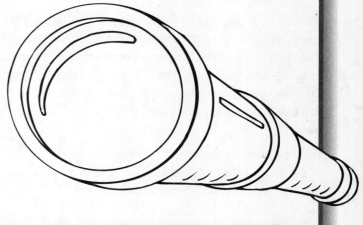

Calling a brave explorer!

He was hired by the Queen of Spain.

Right across the ocean he sailed.

Into the sun and wind and rain.

Bag of Riddles

"I am a large government building. A very important man who makes decisions for our country lives here. What is my name?" Answer: "The White House!" It's fun to guess the names of historic places in or near your community when presented with some brain-teasing riddles. Invite group members to each write two or three riddles about historic places in or around your community with which they are familiar. Tell children that the historic places can be buildings, monuments, parks, museums, and other famous landmarks. When groups finish writing, have them put all the riddles in a paper bag and take turns choosing and reading aloud the riddles for others to guess.

Citizenship

Caring

Showing you care can take many forms. In this exercise, students think about how they can be considerate of others. They make symbols of their thoughtfulness in a clever cutout.

There are hundreds of ways people can show that they care about people, animals, and their environment. Lead your class in a brainstorming session and record their ideas for ways to show that they care about someone or something. For example: "I can show I care about my sister by helping her clean her room. I can show that I care about my friends by comforting them when they are sad. I can show that I care about my classroom by picking up after myself."

Invite group to make Caring Heart Pockets to give to other classes. Ask groups to draw large hearts 12 to 15 inches across on oaktag or poster board and have them cut them out. Then have them use the hearts to draw and cut out another oaktag or poster board heart.

Help them punch holes around the sides and the bottom of both cards, making sure the holes line up with each other. Guide students to make the holes about one inch apart, and about half an inch from the edge. Holes should not be punched in the tops of the hearts, the opening of the pockets.

Model how to thread yarn or ribbon through the holes to stitch the two hearts together. Have students tie a bow at each end.

Groups can then decorate the outsides of their Caring Heart Pockets. On the fronts, they should write something about a caring heart such as "A Caring Heart Is a Beautiful Heart!"

Groups can now refer to the list you made during the brainstorming session. Have them choose items from the list and write them on small squares of construction paper that they can put into the Caring Heart Pockets.

Have your students deliver the Caring Heart Pockets to other classes. There are so many ways to show that you care!

Community Time Capsules

BAMBI

SNOW WHITE

MOTHER GOOSE

Chapter 8 Short-Term Projects

Inventions and transportation take the spotlight as
students roll up their sleeves and get to work on radio ads, time lines,
paintings, dioramas, Morse code bracelets, and more!

Travel Time Line

👤 individual   🕐 20 minutes

Materials: reference books, paper, markers or crayons, old magazines or catalogs, glue, scissors

Let's take a trip back through time! Have children create time lines about travel inventions, beginning with the train, and continuing with the car, airplane, and space shuttle. Provide simple reference books about travel for children to refer to as they create their time lines.

Guide children to write the name of the travel invention, its inventor, the year it was invented, and a few facts about it as they label their time lines. Children can use small cutouts or draw little pictures to illustrate each travel invention. Remind children that they should always list the dates of the inventions in order from earliest to latest.

Important Invention Portraits

👤 individual   🕐 20 minutes

Materials: paper, poster paints and paint brushes, photographs or other visual reference materials (optional)

What invention has made you the most excited? Have students pay tribute to a favorite important invention, such as the telephone, car, computer, or printing press, by painting its portrait. If possible, provide students with photographs or other visual reference materials to help each child render his or her invention's portrait. Ask children to try to include as many details as possible in their portraits. Tell them to leave some space at the bottom of their portraits to write a few lines about how the invention works, and why it is important to their lives. Hang the finished portraits in a classroom Gallery of Inventions.

Travel by Train!

👥 partners   🕐 30 minutes

Materials: paper, pencils, audiocassette recorder (optional)

"Listen up everybody—the Transcontinental Railroad has finally come to Sacramento! All aboard for the ride of your life!" Ask partners to suppose that they are living in a time before trains were common, and the Transcontinental Railroad has just come to town. Then have students write a radio ad encouraging people to buy a train ticket to travel on it.

Elicit from students how they could include information about what a train is, and how train travel can change people's lives. Remind them that a radio ad is a short (thirty-to-forty-five-second) and catchy announcement about a product or a service. Radio ads must use lively language and include important facts that will spark listeners' curiosity. They may use a few sound effects, such as a train whistle or other train sounds. If it's possible, allow partners to use an audiocassette recorder and record their ads.

Morse Code Bracelets

👥 partners   🕐 20 minutes

Materials: Morse Code Bracelets Blackline Master on page 89, construction paper, scissors, markers, tape

Students can make message bracelets written in Morse code! Provide partners with a copy of the blackline master and tell them to use it to write a short message about their community that can be worn on a bracelet. For example: "Our Town Is Great!"

To make the bracelet, have each student cut a 1-by-6-inch strip of construction paper. Then each should write his or her Morse code message on the visible side of the bracelet. Have students write their messages vertically from the strip's top to its bottom and to skip a space after each word of the message. When they finish, partners can exchange bracelets and use the blackline master to translate them.

Remember! Keep working on that Long-Term Project.

Writing Projects

Inventor poems, travel journals, and persuasive speeches
are great ways for your students to explore early inventions
and different kinds of transportation.

What If?

Ask students to imagine what their life would be like if Thomas Edison had never invented the lightbulb, the record player, or the technology for making movies. Brainstorm with them all the ways these inventions impact their lives. Then have each student write a short descriptive letter to Thomas Edison thanking him for his inventions, and telling him what that student's life would be like if he had never become a successful inventor.

All Aboard!

Invite students to imagine a trip they would like to take within the United States. They may look at a map of the United States to give them ideas. Ask them to decide if they would like to take this trip by car, bus, or train. Then have them write three or four entertaining journal entries describing their trip.

Guide students to describe the sights, sounds, and smells of their journeys. Encourage them to include details about the physical environment of the states they are visiting.

Students may illustrate their entries if they wish. Volunteers might want to read their entries to the class.

Saddle Up!

Why should you join the Pony Express? Because it's a great job for the right person! Invite your students to write a speech persuading young men and women to become riders for the Pony Express. Suggest that they include all the positive aspects of the job, such as helping to deliver mail quickly, or the excitement of horseback riding. Encourage students to use descriptive language in their speeches and make the job sound fun. Ask volunteers to give their speeches to the class.

Inventive Inventor Poems

Work with the class to help students choose their favorite inventors. Then have them find partners who have chosen the same inventor and write a poem together about that inventor. Tell children that their poems can be serious or humorous, rhyming or not. Allow time for children to use reference books, such as encyclopedias, in order to get factual information about their inventors. Then model how to use facts in a poem. For example:

Mr. Edison looked around and saw that something was not right.

"It's too dark to read at night," he said, "so I'll invent a light!"

Ask children to use word webs to help them do their prewriting and get ideas for their poems. They may also create lists of rhyming words before they begin to draft their poems.

Invention Unscramble

Have students choose at least three inventions that were popular during the 1940s and write them as scrambled words. Then, tell students to exchange papers with a partner to see if their partner can unscramble the words and list the inventions correctly.

Citizenship

Respect

Respect is earned when people do things to help themselves and help others. This activity awards students for showing respect in and outside of their classroom.

Who deserves respect? You do! Talk with your class about the many things people do to earn the respect of others. Explain that when you respect a person you honor and admire, you treat that person politely and fairly. Challenge the students to brainstorm several examples of situations where a person deserves respect, for example, a person who is not afraid to be different, or who stands up for someone who is being teased by others, or who is polite to his or her classmates, or who has a talent that they share with others.

- Invite partners to create awards of respect to present to each other in a class ceremony. Have each student cut a 6-by-6-inch square of oaktag or thin cardboard and cover it with aluminum foil to make a plaque.

- Then have each student cut a smaller square of construction paper to make a label to glue onto the front of the foil-covered plaque. (Before they glue the label onto the plaque, have students write a few sentences telling why they are presenting this award of respect to their partners.)

- Have students decorate their labels and then glue them onto their plaques.

Hold an Awards of Respect ceremony. Invite partners to come to the front of the class and present each other with their plaques. Have them read the words of their plaques aloud. Guide the class in a round of applause after each award has been presented.

Morse Code Bracelets

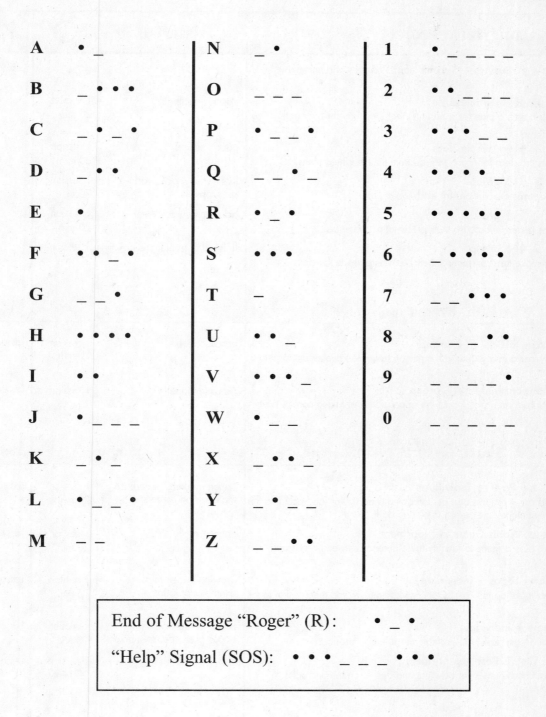

A	• _	**N**	_ •	**1**	• _ _ _ _
B	_ • • •	**O**	_ _ _	**2**	• • _ _ _
C	_ • _ •	**P**	• _ _ •	**3**	• • • _ _
D	_ • •	**Q**	_ _ • _	**4**	• • • • _
E	•	**R**	• _ •	**5**	• • • • •
F	• • _ •	**S**	• • •	**6**	_ • • • •
G	_ _ •	**T**	_	**7**	_ _ • • •
H	• • • •	**U**	• • _	**8**	_ _ _ • •
I	• •	**V**	• • • _	**9**	_ _ _ _ •
J	• _ _ _	**W**	• _ _	**0**	_ _ _ _ _
K	_ • _	**X**	_ • • _		
L	• _ _ •	**Y**	_ • _ _		
M	_ _	**Z**	_ _ • •		

End of Message "Roger" (R):   • _ •

"Help" Signal (SOS):   • • • _ _ _ • • •

Teacher Planner

Long-Term Project pages 92–93	Materials	🕐	Lesson Link
A "Class-y" Business! Students learn the ropes of running a business.			Lessons 1–3
Week 1 👫👫 **whole class** Students create a plan for a business that they may (or may not) carry out.	paper, pencils	1 session 20 min.	
Week 2 👫👫 **whole class** Students list ideas for topics to include in their business plans.	paper, pencils	1 session 30 min.	
Week 3 👫👫 **group** Students write descriptions for each job.	lists from Week 2, various art supplies	1 session 30 min.	
Week 4 👫👫 **group** Students review and polish their presentation materials.	art supplies from Week 3	1 session 20 min.	
Week 5 👫👫 **group** Students take turns presenting their business plans to the class.	finished presentations	1 session 20 min.	

Unit Drama pages 94–99			
Play: Way to Go! 👫👫 **group** Students perform a play about a person going to travel agent to plan a vacation.	props (optional)	1 session 20 min.	Lesson 1
Play: Responsibility 👫👫 **group** Students perform a play about the responsibility of taking care of a pet.	props (optional)	1 session 1 hr.	Lessons 1–3

Chapter 9 Short-Term Projects pages 100–103			
What's My Pay? 👤 **individual** Students draw pictures of a person doing a particular job, including the amount of money the person is paid to do it.	paper, markers*, reference materials on careers	1 session 20 min.	Lesson 1
Needs vs. Wants Game 👫 **partners** Students play a game to identify the difference between needs and wants.	paper, pencils	1 session 20 min.	Lesson 2
Nickname Logos 👤 **individual** Students make up nicknames for their community and then design logos for it.	drawing paper, markers*, examples of logos	1 session 15 min.	Lessons 1–3
Silly Sale 👤 **individual** Students create posters to promote the sale of a product.	poster board or drawing paper, poster paints, markers*	1 session 20 min.	Lesson 2
Which Way is Best 👫 **partners** Students choose a type of business and decide on the best sales method for it.	paper, pencils	1 session 20 min.	Lesson 3

* or crayons

Chapter 9 Writing Projects pages 102–103	Materials	🕐	Lesson Link
A Jolly Good Job! 👤 individual Students write and illustrate the steps involved in doing a particular job.	paper, pencils	1 session 30 min.	Lesson 1
Choices, Choices! 👤 individual Students write stories about someone who has saved money and has to decide how to spend it.	paper, pencils	1 session 20 min.	Lesson 1
Shop Here! 👤 individual Students write descriptive essays about their favorite community businesses.	paper, pencils	1 session 25 min.	Lesson 3
We Can't Do Without It! 👤 individual Students write their opinions about the most important service or product for their community or state.	paper, pencils	1 session 20 min.	Lesson 3
My Business Wish 👤 individual Students write about a kind of business they would like to start and why.	paper, pencils	1 session 20 min.	Lesson 3

Chapter 9 Citizenship Project page 104

	Materials	🕐	Lesson Link
Responsibility 👤👤👤 group Students play the Responsibility Card Game.	scissors, pencils, BLM p. 105	1 session 45 min.	Lessons 1–3

Chapter 10 Short-Term Projects pages 106–107

	Materials	🕐	Lesson Link
"Where Do I Work?" Songs 👤👤👤 group Students write songs related to work that they could teach to the rest of the class.	paper, pencils, audiocassette recorder (optional)	1 session 20 min.	Lesson 1
Lunch Trips 👤👤👤 group Students write menus for typical lunches they might eat.	paper, markers*, encyclopedias (optional)	1 session 20 min.	Lesson 2
Join In! 👤👤 partners Students create posters urging members of their community to join in on a particular project.	poster board, paints and brushes, markers*	1 session 20 min.	Lesson 2
"Cutaway" Mystery Factory 👤 individual Students draw pictures of a product in various stages of its production.	BLM p. 111	1 session 30 min.	Lesson 3
Fascinating Flow Charts 👤👤 partners Students create illustrated flowcharts of a product.	paper, markers*, encyclopedias (optional)	1 session 30 min.	Lesson 3

Chapter 10 Writing Projects pages 108–109

	Materials	🕐	Lesson Link
A Job for You? 👤 individual Students write about jobs that are related to one another.	paper, pencils, reference material on careers	1 session 30 min.	Lesson 1

* or crayons

Chapter 10 **Writing Projects** *continued*	Materials	🕐	Lesson Link
In's and Out's Poems 👤 **individual** Students write poems about the intriguing world of importing and exporting.	paper, pencils	1 session 25 min.	Lessons 1–3
Play Ball 👤 **individual** Students write newspaper articles about famous women in sports or women's athletic teams.	paper, pencils	1 session 20 min.	Lesson 2
It Takes a Lot 👤 **individual** Students write paragraphs about how they imagine goods made it to their classroom.	paper, pencils	1 session 20 min.	Lesson 2
Who Makes Cars? 👤 **individual** Students write biographies of famous car manufacturers.	paper, pencils, reference material on car manufacturers	1 session 30 min.	Lesson 3
Chapter 10 **Citizenship Project** page 110			
Fairness 👥 **group** Students write and prepare skits of public service announcements about fairness.	paper, pencils, video or audio recorder (optional)	1 session 40 min.	Lessons 1–3

NOTES

Long-Term Project

A "Class-y" Business!

What does it take to start a business? It can be as simple as a lemonade stand and some ice cubes or a giant factory with hundreds of machines! Students learn the ropes of running a business in this exciting project.

Brainstorm a Class Business

Week 1

♦♦♦♦ whole class   🕐 20 minutes

Materials: paper, pencils

Tell your students that they are going to create a plan for a business that they may or may not actually start and carry out. To begin, lead students in a brainstorming session about the kinds of businesses the class could start, such as a paper flower-making business, or a car-washing service. List all the responses on the chalkboard and have students copy the list in their notebooks. Then discuss the pros and cons of each type of business. For example, the pros of a paper flower-making business might be that it is easy to obtain colored paper and have the skill to make the flowers. The cons of this business might be that some people prefer to buy fresh flowers rather than paper flowers. Have the class hold a vote and choose the best type of class business.

Explore Topics

Week 2

♦♦♦♦ whole class   🕐 30 minutes

Materials: paper, pencils

Talk with the class about the pertinent topics in a business plan: How to Raise Capital, Supplies, Means of Production, Staffing, Promotion, Selling. Discuss each of the topics in order for students to understand all the parts of a business plan. Work together to get ideas for each topic. For example, how could the class raise the funds necessary to start its business? Where will students find the supplies needed for their business? Who will run the business? Have students list ideas in their notebooks.

OUR START-UP PLAN

Develop a Presentation

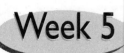 group   30 minutes

Materials: lists from Week 2, art supplies (construction paper, oaktag, clay, scissors, markers, crayons, glue, tape)

Divide the class into groups. Assign each group a separate topic related to the plan for the class business. Ask them to create presentations that will explain their topics. Their presentations should include visual, oral, and written elements. For example, the group who is working on the topic of staffing can create a colorful chart listing all the names of the employees and their specific jobs. The group can then write a short job description for each job. Then volunteers from the group can present the chart to the rest of the class. Guide groups to be creative as well as informative in their presentations. Remind them that they want to generate excitement about the class business through their presentation. Starting a business is hard work, but it can be lots of fun, too!

Continue Creating Presentations

Week 4

group   20 minutes

Materials: art supplies from Week 3

Allow time for students to review and polish their presentation materials. Walk among groups, offering suggestions. Ask groups if they have included all the important details related to their topics. Elicit from students the logic behind their ideas. Ask them to be realistic about what the class can accomplish in their business. Guide them to think about the time and space involved in their business. Help students revise their presentations if necessary.

Give Presentations

Week 5

group   20 minutes

Materials: finished presentations

Ask each group to give its presentation to the rest of the class. Hold the presentations in an order that makes sense. Begin with How to Raise Capital, and move on through Supplies, Means of Production, Staffing, Promotion, and Selling. Remind students to try and make their presentations lively, enthusiastic, and informative. At the start of a business, the people involved are going to work very hard, so they have to really want to do it! Your class may want to use its business plan to actually start a class business. Let's go class!

Way to Go!

When it comes to vacations, the place to start is your local travel agency. Students do the research and then the role-playing!

The Parts: (6 or more players)   • Tina
                    • Narrator   • Agent
                    • Three or more Video Actors

Director's Notes: Talk to your actors about vacations they have taken. Talk about places where they would like to go on vacation. Select three places Tina must choose from for her family's vacation. Your group will need to gather information about these places from each other or from research. Decide what you will show about each of the places during the scenario's improvisation. **_Improv Directions_** and blank spaces show where the actors should improvise.

Narrator:	Congratulations, Tina. It's your turn to decide where the family will go on vacation.
Tina:	I'm so excited. **_(Improv Directions:_** _List three places.)_
Narrator:	All three trips sound fun and interesting.
Tina:	That's the problem. How will I ever decide?
Narrator:	If you want to make a good decision you'll need to gather information.
Agent:	I can help with that.
Tina:	Who are you?
Agent:	I'm a travel agent. It's my job to give people information about vacations.

Tina:	Can you tell me what there is to do and see at each of these places?
Agent:	I can do better than that. These videos can show you everything you want to know. Watch them and picture yourself in each place.
	*(**Improv Directions:** Video Actors improvise the three videos. Tina learns about each place as she supposes what it would be like to go there. She might even find herself drawn into the video improvisation.)*
Narrator:	Well, Tina, are you ready to make a decision?
Tina:	I think so. I know what my choices are. I gathered information about my choices. And I've imagined what could happen for each choice I might make. Yes, I'm ready to decide.
Narrator:	Where do you want to go?
Tina:	I want to go to _____, because *(**Improv Directions:** Give reasons for her decision.)*
Narrator:	Way to go, Tina! Have a great time on your vacation.

Responsibility

What does it take to be a pet owner?
Fred, and your students, are about to find out!

The Parts: (4 players)
- Narrator   • Mom
- Fred   • Dad

Director's Notes: Before doing this play think about how you want to block it. *Blocking* is where the actors stand and move onstage during the play. Experiment with where you ask your actors to stand. Sometimes you might want them to face each other. This would show your audience the characters are in the same scene. Sometimes you might want a character to face away from the others. This could show that the character is not in that scene. At the end of this play a dog is barking. See who has the most convincing dog bark in your class!

Narrator:	Like most boys his age Fred wanted a puppy.
Fred:	If I had a puppy I'd name him Mac. We'd be best friends.
Narrator:	Fred wanted a puppy more than anything in the world. He asked his parents if he could have a puppy. They said—
Mom & Dad:	No.
Narrator:	But Fred just couldn't stop thinking about Mac. He tried to convince his father.
Fred:	A dog could guard the house.
Dad:	We have an alarm system.
Narrator:	He talked to his mother.
Fred:	Don't you think puppies are cute?
Mom:	Not as cute as you are Fred.
Fred:	Oh come on now, Mom.
Narrator:	No matter what Fred said his parents told him—

Mom & Dad:	No.
Dad:	A puppy is a big responsibility.
Mom:	It has to be fed.
Dad:	It has to be walked.
Mom:	It has to be house broken.
Fred:	I'll do all those things.
Dad:	You're too young.
Fred:	I'm not. I'll be very responsible.
Mom:	Isn't that what you said when you got a paper route?
Fred:	Yes.
Mom:	And what happened?
Fred:	I overslept and forgot to deliver the papers.
Dad:	And didn't you say you'd be responsible when you borrowed my camera?
Fred:	Yes.
Dad:	And what happened?
Fred:	I lost it. But I'm older now. I'm more responsible.
Mom:	Fred, a dog is more important than a camera or a paper route.
Dad:	It's a living being. You couldn't lose it or forget about it.
Fred:	I won't. Please, Mom. Please, Dad. I promise to be responsible.
Narrator:	Fred talked, and pleaded, and begged his parents. Finally they said—
Mom & Dad:	All right.
Dad:	Prove that you are responsible.
Mom:	Then you can have a puppy.
Fred:	I will, I promise. What do I have to do?

Responsibility *continued*

Narrator:	Fred's father handed him a potted houseplant.
Dad:	Take care of this.
Fred:	What's this?
Mom:	An ivy plant. You'll need to water it and make sure it gets enough sunlight.
Fred:	I can do that.
Dad:	You'll also have to walk it.
Fred:	Walk it?
Dad:	To practice taking care of a dog, you'll have to walk this plant.
Mom:	Puppies need to be walked three times a day.
Dad:	That means getting up early before school to walk your plant— I mean puppy.
Mom:	That means coming straight home from school before playing with your friends.
Dad:	It means missing your favorite television show after dinner.
Mom:	If you can do all that for one week, you can have a puppy.
Dad:	Is it a deal?
Fred:	Mom and Dad, it's a deal.
Narrator:	All week Fred worked very hard to be responsible.
Dad:	Good morning, Fred.
Fred:	Good morning, Dad.
Dad:	You're up early.
Fred:	I've got to walk Ivy before school.

Narrator: When his friends asked him to play ball after school Fred told them he couldn't.

Fred: I have to go home and walk my plant— I mean, oh never mind. I'll explain it later.

Narrator: By the end of the week Fred had a good idea of what it means to be responsible.

Mom: This plant never looked better.

Fred: I took care of it the best I could.

Dad: You've done a very good job, Fred.

Mom: We're proud of you.

Dad: Do you still want a puppy?

Fred: More than ever.

Mom: In that case you better go outside.

Dad: There's someone who wants to meet you.

(A barking dog is heard.)

Fred: It's Mac! Mom, Dad, thank you, thank you, thank you!

Narrator: From that day on, Fred, Mac, and Ivy were best friends.

Short-Term Projects

Students find out that businesses require creativity when they design logos and other promotional tools.

Which Way Is Best?

👥 partners 🕐 20 minutes

Materials: paper, pencils

Create two lists of different kinds of businesses on the chalkboard: one for Goods and one for Services. For example, the Goods list might include shoes, snacks, pets, and T-shirts. The Services list might include car wash, baby-sitting, pet care, and elder care. Invite students to add their own ideas to the lists. Then discuss the various ways that these goods and services can be sold, such as via retail stores, mail-order companies, Web sites, door-to-door sales, and so on.

Ask partners to choose one type of business from the list and decide on the best sales method for it. Then have them write a plan that promotes their idea. The best method of sales for a car wash, for instance, might be flyers that are handed out door-to-door or put on the windshields of cars in the neighborhood.

Have partners share and discuss their sales plan with the class.

Remember! Keep working on that Long-Term Project.

Needs vs. Wants Game

👥 partners 🕐 20 minutes

Materials: paper, pencils

Partners can play this identification game at their seats. Have each partner write a list of school needs and school wants. Guide the students to vary the order of needs and wants on their lists. A sample list might look as follows: chairs, desks, swimming pool, teachers, new computers, paper. When each partner has written between ten and twenty needs and wants, the partners should take turns quietly reading their lists aloud to each other. The first child reads his or her list in the order it was written, and the partner marks down an *N* for Need and a *W* for Want corresponding to what is read on the list. The partner can then check the letters he or she wrote against the list to see if all the Needs and Wants were correctly identified.

Nickname Logos

♦ individual   🕐 15 minutes

Materials: drawing paper, markers or crayons, examples of logos (optional)

New York City is the Big Apple; Chicago is the Windy City. Does your community have a nickname? If so, invite your students to create logos to use with the nickname. If not, have the students make up nicknames for your community and then design the logos. Remind students that a logo is a simple, eye-catching design. Tell students that logos are often drawn boldly and do not include a lot of details. If possible, provide students with examples of successful logos for them to use as inspiration. Then hang students' finished work in a community classroom display area.

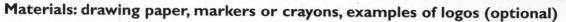

Silly Sale!

♦ individual   🕐 20 minutes

Materials: poster board or drawing paper; poster paints, markers or crayons

"Pickles for sale! Secret message in each jar! Win a trip around the world!" Ask your students to think of fun or silly ways to promote the sale of a product as Homer Price did in the story *The Doughnuts*. Then have them create exciting posters for it. Tell them that their product can be real or made up. Challenge them to come up with creative ways to make people want to buy ordinary products. People might buy a particular brand of paper towels if they thought a toy was hidden inside the cardboard tube!

What's My Pay?

♦ individual   🕐 20 minutes

Materials: paper, markers or crayons, reference materials for careers (optional)

Provide a list of different jobs and invite each student to choose one. For example: baby-sitter, police officer, mayor, librarian, secretary, dog-walker. Students can research or guess how much money the jobs they chose will pay, either by the hour, the day, the week, or the year. Then ask each student to draw a picture of a person doing the job. Have each student label the picture with the name of the job and the amount of money the person is paid to do it. For example, a dog-walker might make $5.00 per hour. If that dog-walker worked four hours a week, he or she would make $20.00 per week.

Writing Projects

Chapter 9

Big business inspires big fun in these varied writing projects.
Invite your students to dream up businesses, "job" haikus, stories about choices,
and other wise words about the fascinating world of work.

We Can't Do Without It!

What's the most important product or service your community or state turns out? Is your state known for its delicious cheeses? Does your community have an historic movie theater that people come from miles around to attend? Invite students to research or guess the most important service or product for their community or state and write short opinion pieces about their findings. Remind students to use facts or examples to back up their opinions. Volunteers may want to read their opinions to the class.

A Jolly Good Job!

What are the jobs of your students? Do they do chores in class or at home? Do they run errands for neighbors? Ask students to brainstorm jobs they know how to do. Then have them write and illustrate the steps in sequence for doing these jobs. If the job is shoveling snow, for example, the first step might be to dress appropriately for the weather. The next step might be gathering supplies such as gloves and a shovel. Guide students to be clear and to visualize each step before they write it down.

My Business Wish

Who hasn't dreamed of being the president of a successful business? Invite your students to close their eyes and suppose they are the owners of great businesses. Perhaps one business makes wonderful toys that are priced so low everyone in the world can buy them. Maybe a business offers a service that is so popular, customers call their orders in all day and night! Have students write about what kinds of businesses they would like to start and why. Encourage them to illustrate their work and share it with the class.

Choices, Choices!

Invite students to write stories about someone who has saved up a certain amount of money and has to decide what to do with it. Will the person save it? Spend part and save part? What might the person buy? Ask students to create lists of ideas for their stories before they begin to write. Have each student choose the best idea from his or her list and begin to draft the story. When students finish writing, have them look over their stories and see if there are things they want to add or change. Are there enough descriptive details in the story? Is it clear why the person has to make a choice? Is the person making an easy choice or a difficult choice? Finally, have students revise and share their stories.

Shop Here!

Ask students if they have favorite stores or businesses in their community. Do they like to eat at a particular pizza parlor or ice cream shop? Do they favor a certain shopping center or movie theater? Have students write short, descriptive essays about their favorite community businesses. Ask them to include their opinions about the businesses, as well as some details that support their opinions. Guide them to write their essays for readers who have never visited the businesses described.

Citizenship

Responsibility

Business owners must be very responsible! They have many different tasks to accomplish, and people count on them. This fun card game encourages students to think responsibly about business.

Brainstorm with the class about the different ways that a business owner has to be responsible. Guide the class to see that a business owner must be responsible to himself or herself, to his or her family, to the business itself and the business property, to the employees, the suppliers, the customers, and the community.

Hand out copies of the Responsibility Card Game Blackline Master to the class. Have each student cut apart the cards and draw a picture that goes with the category on each of the cards. Then break students into groups, and have each group categorize their cards according to type, making a stack for each category.

Show each group how to make a Category Card. Cut an 8-by-8-inch square of oaktag. Divide it into three rows of three squares each.

Have students write one of the following words in each of the squares on their Category Card: Self, Family, Business, Property, Employees, Suppliers, Customers, Community. In the ninth square, students should write Wild Card!

To play the game, have students take turns tossing a counter onto the Category Card. When the counter lands on a category, the student must choose a card from that category stack and explain how a business owner can be responsible to whomever or whatever is listed on the card. If the category is Property, for example, the student may say that a business owner can be responsible to the business property by sweeping its floors to keep it clean. If the student answers to the group's satisfaction, the student may keep the card. If the counter lands on the Wild Card the student may choose a card from any category. Play continues until all of the category card stacks are empty.

Social Studies Plus!

Responsibility Card Game

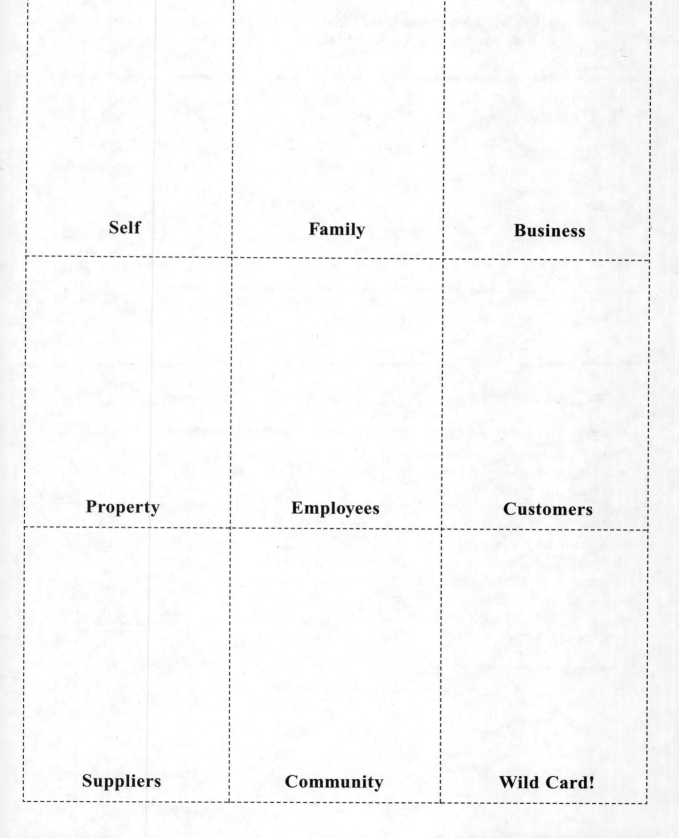

Self	Family	Business
Property	**Employees**	**Customers**
Suppliers	**Community**	**Wild Card!**

Short-Term Projects

Your students will love to work on these engaging projects that take on the production of goods—from natural resources to world interdependence!

"Cutaway" Mystery Factory

👤 individual   🕐 30 minutes

Materials: "Cutaway" Mystery Factory Blackline Master (page 111), pencils

Hand out copies of the blackline master to students. Tell them that the cutaway diagram shows the inside of a factory for a mysterious product. Have students think about any products they like that could be made on the assembly line shown in this factory. Then have them write descriptions of each of the numbered production steps on the blanks. Encourage them to be fanciful. What is the mystery product?

Remember! Keep working on that Long-Term Project.

Fascinating Flow Chart

👥 partners   🕐 30 minutes

Materials: paper, crayons or markers, encyclopedias (optional)

Invite partners to create an illustrated flowchart. Explain that the flowchart will show the production of a product from raw material or crop to how it looks when it is ready for sale. On the chalkboard, model how to illustrate and use arrows to create a flowchart. A flowchart for the production of popcorn would follow this sequence: a kernel of corn, the sprouting corn plant, the larger corn stalk ready for harvest, the corn cob being shucked, the corn being removed and put onto a tray to dry, the corn being popped in a pan, the popcorn being put into a bag, the bag put in a box, the box driven to a grocery store. Students may use reference materials, such as encyclopedias, if available. Otherwise, challenge students to suppose the steps of production for their product.

"Where Do I Work?" Songs

👥👤 group   🕐 20 minutes

Materials: paper, pencils, audio cassette recorder (optional)

Have each group write a song, related to work, that they could teach to the rest of the class. If possible, allow groups to record their songs on an audiocassette player and make their own work "soundtrack." Suggest that groups set their songs to familiar tunes. For example, they may substitute the phrase "I've been cooking in the kitchen," for the first line of "I've Been Working on the Railroad." Students can then continue on with lyrics related to the job of cooking. When groups finish, allow time for them to perform each song for the rest of the class before they teach or record it.

Lunch Trips

👥👤 group   🕐 20 minutes

Materials: paper, markers or crayons, encyclopedias (optional)

Ask your students: Where do the foods in your lunch come from? Remind them that before foods are bought in the school cafeteria or in a grocery store, they are grown somewhere and then shipped either by boat, truck, or plane. Ask groups to write menus for typical lunches they might eat. If possible, provide groups with encyclopedias and have them research where all the food in their menus might come from. Then have them create illustrated charts showing where each menu item is from. If no reference material is available, challenge students to guess where each food item might have been grown.

Join In!

👤👤 partners   🕐 20 minutes

Materials: poster board; poster paints and brushes, markers, or crayons

Have partners think up a project for their community. To get them started, have them jot down all the things they can think of that their community might need or want. Then guide them to create a poster urging the members of their community to join in the project. Suggest that students use their posters to point out that people depend on one another to get things done. For example, one community project might be to create a park in the business district for workers and shoppers to enjoy. The poster might focus on all the ways in which the community members can contribute to something that will benefit everyone.

Chapter 10 Writing Projects

Importing and exporting, sports, and car manufacturing are some of the engaging topics that students write about in these multi-faceted projects.

It Takes a Lot!

Ask students to imagine what their school would be like without books, desks, and chairs. What do they think are the steps involved in getting a book or a desk from its raw form—wood from a tree, for example—to a product they use every day in school. Tell the students to write a paragraph about how they imagine one of those goods made it to their classroom. They may illustrate their paragraphs if they wish. Guide students to check the organization of their paragraphs to see if there is a clear beginning, middle, and end.

A Job for You?

Jobs, jobs, jobs. Some jobs require workers to specialize in a particular skill and others require more general skills.

Have partners compare and contrast two different jobs. One partner can research a specialized job, and the other partner can research a generalized job. If possible, have partners write about jobs that are related to one another. In baseball bat production, for instance, a worker might specialize in sanding the baseball bats, while another worker might perform the more generalized job of selling the baseball bats in a sporting goods store.

If they are available, provide encyclopedias or other reference books about careers for students to use in their research. Suggest that students write the sequence of steps each worker must go through in order to do his or her job. When students finish writing, have them compare and contrast the two jobs.

In's and Out's Poem

Invite your students to write poems about the intriguing world of importing and exporting. Prompt students: Where do goods come from? Where do they go? Beautiful treasures are shipped to and from distant lands. Think of the long journeys these goods must make! Explain that students' poems may rhyme or not and may be funny or serious. For example:

> Tea from China makes quite a trip
> Serve cold or hot, then take a sip!
> In a kettle, in a cup
> It traveled far, so drink it up!

Encourage students to illustrate their poems.

Play Ball!

Ask students to write short newspaper articles about famous women in sports or women's athletic teams. Encourage them to write eye-catching headlines and to answer the questions Who? What? Where? When? How? and Why? in their articles. Students may also create "photographs" to accompany their articles. If desired, staple students' work together and create a Women in Sports Newspaper.

Who Makes Cars?

Who makes the cars we drive in? There have been a lot of car manufacturers since Henry Ford invented his Model T. Ask students to research car manufacturers and to write short biographies about them. Provide encyclopedias or reference books to students and guide them to jot down the important facts of their subjects' lives. Each biography should note when and where the person was born, details about his or her childhood, when the person developed an interest in cars or business, and a little history about his or her experience as a car manufacturer. Students may wish to illustrate the events of their subjects' lives.

Chapter 10
Citizenship

Fairness

Playing fair is a great way to play! But how can we get everyone to understand that? How about an inspiring public service announcement?

Elicit from the class that a public service announcement is a television or radio spot that tells people an important message. Talk with the students about public service announcements they have seen, such as the public service announcement asking people to "Keep America Beautiful" by not littering.

Brainstorm ideas for public service announcements about fairness. Record students' responses in a list on the chalkboard. Then divide the class into groups and have each group choose an idea that it likes from the list. Invite each group to create a public service announcement based on its idea.

Tell groups that they may write speeches or act out skits in order to get their messages across. Then allow time for groups to write and rehearse their ideas.

Have groups perform their public service announcements. If possible, record their work with a video camera or an audiocassette recorder. Groups' public service announcements can then be played for other classes.

"Cutaway" Mystery Factory

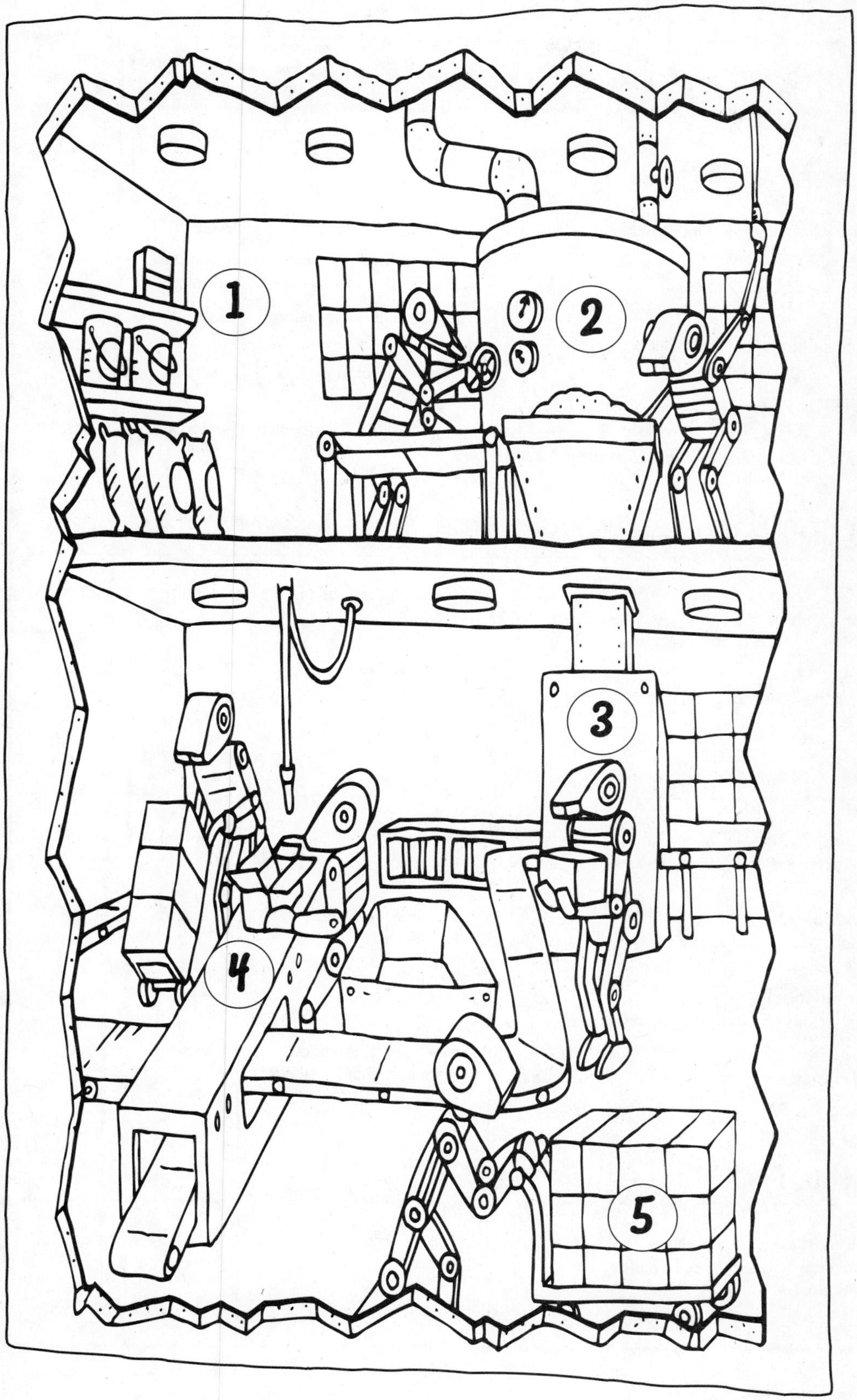

1. _____

   _____

   _____

2. _____

   _____

   _____

   _____

3. _____

   _____

   _____

4. _____

   _____

   _____

   _____

5. _____

   _____

   _____

Long-Term Project pages 114–115	Materials	🕐	Lesson Link
Class Council Students design an election campaign and run for office.			Lesson 2
Week 1 👪 **whole class** Students brainstorm the areas of classroom life that need to be governed.	paper, pencils	1 session 20 min.	
Week 2 👪 **whole class** Students assign jobs for the Class Council campaign.	list from Week 1, paper, pencils	1 session 20 min.	
Weeks 3 & 4 👪 **group** Students work on their campaign slogans and speeches.	paper, pencils, posterboard, various art supplies	1 session 30 min.	
Week 5 👪 **group** Students present their campaigns.	finished campaign posters and buttons	1 session 30 min.	
Week 6 👪 **whole class** Students create a ballot box and enter votes for Class Council members.	BLM p. 127, scissors, pencils	1 session 30 min.	

Unit Drama pages 116–121			
Play: Freedom Walk 👪 **group** Students perform a play about a time in history when African Americans were treated differently than other Americans.	props, costumes (optional)	1 session 1 hr.	Lessons 1–3
Scenarios: Good Citizens! 👪 **group** Students perform skits about the traits that good citizens share.	props (optional)	1 session 20 min.	Lesson 3

Chapter 11 Short-Term Projects pages 122–123			
Terrific Taxes 👤 **individual** Students design public service posters explaining how taxes help pay for things the community needs.	paper, markers*	1 session 20 min.	Lesson 1
Capital Scenes 👤 **individual** Students use the blackline master to draw in scenes they think might have taken place in each location.	BLM p. 133, colored pencils, reference material (optional)	1 session 30 min.	Lesson 2
Report It! Cartoons 👤 **individual** Students create four-panel cartoons about a reporter on the scene.	paper, markers*	1 session 20 min.	Lesson 2
Presidential Figures 👤 **individual** Students create cardboard cutouts of a president, including some details about his life.	poster board, reference material on U.S. presidents, art supplies	1 session 20 min.	Lesson 2

Chapter 11 Writing Projects pages 124–125			
What's My Point? 👤 **individual** Students write paragraphs about taxes from both the taxpayers' and the government's point of view.	paper, pencils	1 session 30 min.	Lesson 1

* or crayons

Chapter 11 Writing Projects continued	Materials	🕐	Lesson Link
Pilgrim Poems 🧍 individual Students write poems from the point of view of a Pilgrim.	paper, pencils	1 session 20 min.	Lesson 1
A Class Pledge 🧍 individual Students discuss the Pledge of Allegiance, and then write their own classroom pledges.	paper, pencils, copy of the Pledge of Allegiance	1 session 20 min.	Lessons 1–3
What Do You Do? 🧍 individual Students write letters to a community government official.	paper, pencils, list of community gov't members	1 session 30 min.	Lesson 2

Chapter 11 Citizenship Project page 126			
Caring 🧍🧍🧍 whole class Students paint a mural showing the ways people care for their community.	paper, pencils, poster paints and brushes, butcher paper	1 session 45 min.	Lesson 3

Chapter 12 Short-Term Projects pages 128–129			
"Good Government" Mobile 🧍🧍 partners Students create mobiles about good government practices.	hangers, markers*, holepunch, string, oaktag, scissors	1 session 30 min.	Lesson 1
Piece of the Pie 🧍 individual Students draw pie charts showing various government service categories.	chart paper, markers*	1 session 20 min.	Lesson 1
Vice-President Cards 🧍🧍 partners Students create fact-file cards on United States vice presidents.	index cards, shoebox, markers*, encyclopedias	1 session 20 min.	Lessons 1–3
Help Out! 🧍 individual Students create posters to enlist people in a school-cleaning project.	poster board, markers*	1 session 20 min.	Lesson 2

Chapter 12 Writing Projects pages 130–131			
The Magic of Myths 🧍 individual Students write myths about the founding of their community.	paper, pencils	1 session 30 min.	Lessons 1–3
If I Ruled the World 🧍 individual Students write summaries of the most important things they would do if they ruled the world.	paper, pencils	1 session 20 min.	Lessons 1–3
Simulation: Public Service Announcement 🧍 individual Students write a public service announcement requesting that people attend a town meeting.	paper, pencils	1 session 30 min.	Lesson 2
"Cleanup" Jingles 🧍🧍🧍 group Students write radio jingles about a community cleanup project.	paper, pencils	1 session 20 min.	Lesson 3

Chapter 12 Citizenship Project page 132			
Honesty 🧍🧍🧍 whole class Students design and create Honesty Badges that they can hand out to people who speak or behave honestly.	paper, pencils, markers*, ribbon, glue or stapler	1 session 40 min.	Lessons 2–3

* or crayons

NOTES

NOTES

Unit 6 Long-Term Project

Class Council

Do you need help governing the classroom? Call a meeting of the Class Council! Here's a chance for students to design an election campaign, come up with slogans, and run for office!

Plan a Class Council

Week 1

👤👤👤 whole class   🕐 20 minutes

Materials: paper, pencils

A classroom is like a community—each has rules and leaders in order to make sure everything runs smoothly.

1. Tell students that they are going to establish a class council to help their class meet its needs. Brainstorm about the different areas of classroom life.

2. Prompt students by writing this list on the chalkboard: classroom behavior, classroom work, classroom chores, and special events.

Choose Jobs

Week 2

👤👤👤 whole class   🕐 20 minutes

Materials: list from Week 1, paper, pencils

Write this list on the chalkboard: council members, campaign managers, publicity people. Explain to students that a campaign manager works with the publicity people to help design posters, buttons, and slogans. The council member will write and give speeches. Have each student decide which job he or she would like.

Divide students into groups. Assign each candidate at least one campaign manager and one publicity person. In the election, two candidates can run for Commissioner of Classroom Behavior, two candidates can run for Commissioner of Classroom Work, and so on.

Vote for Pat O'Hare She's There She's Fair

Social Studies Plus!

Developing a Campaign

Week 3 & 4

group **30 minutes**

Materials: paper, pencils, poster board, oaktag, scissors, markers, poster paints, crayons

Have groups work on slogans for their campaign. For example, a slogan for the candidate running for Commissioner of Classroom Behavior might be, "I will make sure everyone respects each other!" Have groups talk about all the things their candidates will do if they are elected to the Class Council. Groups should list their ideas. Then the candidates should write short speeches saying why they should be elected. The campaign manager and the publicity people will work together to create "buttons" and posters.

Have the group members look over their work. Campaign managers and publicity people should read the candidates' speeches and make suggestions. Candidates should make sure the posters and buttons match the ideas in their speeches. Walk among groups offering suggestions. Ask a volunteer to decorate and label a shoe box in order to create a Ballot Box.

Present Campaigns

Week 5

group **30 minutes**

Materials: finished campaign posters and buttons

Ask each group to present its campaign. Hang posters, hand out buttons, and allow time for each candidate to make his or her speech. Suggest that candidates read expressively. Invite students to ask the candidates questions about what they will do if they are elected.

Hold Elections

Week 6

whole class **30 minutes**

Materials: blackline master (page 127), scissors, pencils

Hand out copies of the blackline master to students. Have them cut out the ballot slips and write the name of the office and the name of the candidate they are voting for. Tell them not to show their ballot slips to anyone. Have them fold their slips in half and drop them into the ballot box. When all the votes are in, have a volunteer open the box and read the names. Another volunteer can tally the number of votes for each candidate on the chalkboard. Once the results are in, it's up to you if you want to lead the Class Council to make good on all their campaign promises!

Good Citizens!

Students have learned that good citizens demonstrate caring, respect, responsibility, fairness, honesty, and courage.

Students will work in groups of two. They will improvise scenes that illustrate good citizenship. Allow students time to discuss which aspect of good citizenship they would like to demonstrate. Then give them a few minutes to decide upon a situation for their improvisation. Here are some examples to get students thinking.

Character Traits

Caring: Students could improvise a scene where two volunteers collect money for the fight against cancer.

Respect: Students could improvise a scene where two people demonstrate good manners, such as holding doors for each other or using polite language such as "please" and "thank you."

Responsibility: Students could improvise a scene showing people recycling, or helping to keep the community clean.

Fairness: Students could improvise a scene where they share a toy or meal.

Honesty: Students could improvise a scene where they return money given to them by mistake.

Courage: Students could improvise a scene where they stand up for a strongly held belief.

Share these ideas with students. Encourage them to make suggestions of their own.

After each improvisation, ask the class to guess which good citizenship trait was shown. When every student has completed an improvisation, ask the class why these traits are important.

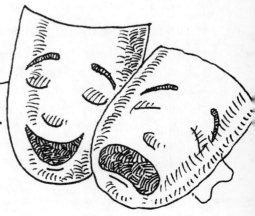

Freedom Walk

Have you ever been treated unfairly? How did it make you feel? This play is about a time in our history when African Americans were treated differently from other Americans. It's a play about how they made things better.

The Parts: (11 players)
- Three Narrators
- A Family (Sally, Dad, Tom, Mama)
- Dr. King
- Man
- Bus Drive
- Rosa Parks

> **Director's Notes:** In this play the character Rosa Parks has only one line. In fact, she speaks only one word. But it is a very important part. Remind the actor playing Rosa that she must act even when she is not speaking. Ask her how she would feel if a strange man were yelling at her to give him her seat. Tell her that sometimes silence speaks louder than words. Ask her to show bravery in the way she sits and finally speaks.

Narrator 1: This is a story about a girl named Sally.

Sally: *(excited, holding up an invitation)* Mama, look what I got!

Narrator 2: No, this is a story about Dr. Martin Luther King, Jr.

Dr. King: *(preaching to a crowd)* Freedom is not free.

Narrator 3: Wait a minute. Yes, this story is about Sally, and Dr. King, and a lot of other people. But this story starts with a woman named Rosa Parks.

(Rosa Parks is sitting on a bus.)

Narrator 1: Is that her?

Narrator 3: Yes, she just got off from work.

Narrator 2: Miss Parks looks tired.

Narrator 3: She's a seamstress and she's worked very hard today.

Man: Get up.

Narrator 1: Why is that man telling her to get up?

Freedom Walk *continued*

Narrator 3: Because it's 1955 in Montgomery, Alabama. In the South at that time, if a white person told an African American to give up their seat on the bus, they did.

Narrator 2: Was that legal?

Narrator 3: No it wasn't. It's just the way things were.

Man: Are you deaf? I said get up.

Bus Driver: What's the problem over there?

Man: She won't give up her seat.

Bus Driver: Girl, if you don't listen I'll have to call the police. Will you get up?

Rosa: *(proudly, calmly)* No.

Narrator 1: What happened?

Narrator 3: They arrested Miss Parks and put her in jail.

Narrator 1: Now I see why you say this is where our story starts. But I think it's time we got to the part about Sally.

Narrator 3: That's a good idea.

Narrator 1: There she is with her parents and her brother, Tom.

Sally: Daddy, have you seen my party invitation?

Dad: Yes, Sally, it's very nice. *(Pause)* When is this party?

Sally: This Saturday at one o'clock. See, Daddy, it says so right here on the card. Isn't the card pretty?

Dad: Yes, it's very pretty. Where does Jill live?

Mama: Over at Elm and First Street.

Dad: That's about four miles away.

Mama: Why? Is something wrong?

Dad: I don't think Sally can go to this party.

Sally: Daddy, I've got to go. Jill is my best friend. I'm giving her a music box for a present.

Social Studies Plus!

Dad:	I know, sweetie, but you've heard about Miss Parks.
Mama:	Oh no, what's happened now?
Dad:	She's fine. She's out of jail.
Mama:	Thank goodness.
Sally:	What does Miss Parks have to do with Jill's party?
Dad:	People are very upset about what happened to Miss Parks. They're upset that any of us should be forced to give up our seats.
Tom:	It makes me very angry.
Mama:	Tom!
Dad:	Son, you only hurt yourself when you let your anger take over. Do you understand?
Tom:	Maybe.
Dad:	Anyway, people think it's time we did something about this situation.
Tom:	Are we going to fight?
Dad:	In a way. We're going to boycott the buses.
Sally:	Boycott? What does that mean?
Dad:	It means that we won't ride the buses.
Mama:	When does the boycott start?
Dad:	Tomorrow.
Sally:	But if we don't ride the buses, how will we get anywhere? How will you get to work, Daddy?
Dad:	Just like everyone else, I'll walk.
Sally:	Then I'll walk to Jill's party.
Mama:	It's too far for you, Sally. You'll have to stay home.
Sally:	I've got to go. Can't I boycott after the party?
Dad:	No, Sally. If just one of us rides the buses it will break the boycott. Do you understand?
Sally:	Sort of. But I have to give Jill her present.
Tom:	She doesn't understand anything.

Freedom Walk *continued*

Dad:	And neither do you. Tomorrow night Dr. King is speaking. We're all going to listen and learn.
Narrator 2:	Finally, we're getting to the part about Dr. King.
Narrator 3:	That's right. Tell us about him.
Narrator 2:	Dr. King was a local minister. He became the head of the boycott. He was a very good speaker and hundreds of people came to hear him.
Dr. King:	Brothers and sisters, these are dark days in Montgomery. Our people are treated unkindly. We are not respected. At times we even fear for our safety and our lives. There are some people who hate us. But we cannot allow ourselves to hate others.
Dad:	Listen to this, Tom.
Dr. King:	As hard as it may seem we must meet hate with love. We must meet hate with kindness and goodness. Hate also hurts the hater.
Dad:	Do you understand?
Tom:	Yes, Daddy.
Dr. King:	What we can do is stand together. And we should remember that we are not alone. There are many good white people who stand with us. So until we are treated with the respect that all people deserve, we will not ride the buses. We will boycott for as long as it takes.
Narrator 1:	*(cheering)* Boycott, boycott . . .
Narrator 2:	*(joining the cheering)* Boycott, boycott, boycott . . .
Narrator 3:	*(joining in)* Boycott, boycott, boycott . . .
	(Tom and his father join in the chanting.)
Tom and Dad:	Boycott, boycott, boycott . . .
Mama:	Do you understand now, Sally?
Sally:	Yes, Mama. But I still want to go to Jill's party.
Mama:	I know, sweetie. I have an idea. *(She whispers in Sally's ear.)*

Sally:	Boycott, boycott, BOYCOTT!
Narrator 2:	That night the cheering went on for a long time.
Narrator 3:	The next day was Saturday, the day of Jill's party.
Narrator 1:	Tom and his Dad woke up to the smell of pancakes cooking.
Tom:	What's the special occasion?
Mama:	Sit down and have some breakfast, son, and then put on your walking shoes.
Sally:	We're all going to walk to Jill's party.
Mama:	We're joining the boycott! (***Improv Directions:** Show the family getting ready to walk. Then show them going out into the streets. They could be joined, one by one, by other neighbors. You might try to get members of the audience to join you. In the end, many people could be walking together, holding hands. They could sing a song from the civil rights movement, such as "We Shall Overcome." The song should be sung joyously.*)
Narrator 1:	So you see, this story was about Sally.
Narrator 2:	And about Dr. King.
Narrator 3:	And about a brave woman named Rosa Parks.
Narrator 1:	How long did the boycott last?
Narrator 3:	For over a year the people walked everywhere.
Narrator 2:	Did it work?
Narrator 3:	It certainly did. Because of the boycott African Americans no longer had to give up their seats to whites. Eventually, the Civil Rights Bill was passed.

Have your students explore the diverse layers of community government—cartoons, posters, clay figures, and story boards that keep students engaged!

Terrific Taxes

👤 individual   🕐 20 minutes

Materials: paper, markers or crayons

Can taxes be terrific? Absolutely! Especially when they pay for things a community needs and wants, such as roads, parks, firefighters, and more. With your class, brainstorm a list of goods and services that are paid for with taxes. Then have each student choose an item from the list and design a public service poster explaining how taxes help support the item.

Guide students to be creative and colorful as well as informative. Who likes taxes? Everybody who gets to play in the town swimming pool!

Capital Scenes

👤 individual   🕐 30 minutes

Materials: Capital Happenings Blackline Master (page 133), colored pencils, reference material (optional)

Hand out copies of the blackline master to students. Have students draw in a scene that they think might have happened or could happen in or near each location on the blackline master. Suggest that they write speech balloons for the characters in their scenes. For example, in the White House scene, a student could draw a picture of President Adams moving in with his family. His speech balloon might say: "I am President John Adams. My family and I were the first people to live in the White House."

Provide students with reference material about U.S. presidents, and the government buildings, monuments, and landmarks located in our nation's capital in order to help them get ideas.

Report It! Cartoons

Materials: paper, markers or crayons

Have students draw and write four-panel cartoons about a reporter who is on the scene during an exciting moment in the history of civil rights. For example, have them imagine they are news reporters who were there when Rosa Parks refused to give up her seat on the bus. Have students answer the questions Who? What? Where? When? and Why? in their cartoons. Remind them that a reporter is like a narrator who is summarizing a story for listeners.

Remember! Keep working on that Long-Term Project.

Presidential Figures

🚶 individual   🕐 20 minutes

Materials: poster board or thin cardboard, craft sticks, tape, markers or crayons, scissors, clay, reference material about U.S. presidents

When you think of George Washington, do you also picture Mt. Vernon and a cherry tree? Have each student choose a U.S. president and research some details about that president's life. Then have students create cardboard cutouts of the presidents they chose and a couple of objects or locations related to each president. Students can tape their cutouts onto craft sticks.

Have them place the bottom ends of each craft stick into a small square of modeling clay so the cutouts will stand up. Create a U.S. president display in your class. Have each student share information about his or her chosen president with the rest of the class.

Writing Projects

Students try their hands at writing Pilgrim poems, classroom pledges, point-of-view essays, and letters to town officials!

A Class Pledge

The Pledge of Allegiance is a powerful piece of writing.

1. Hand out copies of it to your students. Read it together with students and then have a volunteer summarize its meaning. Discuss why United States citizens stand and face the flag while they recite it.

2. Then invite partners to write a new "pledge of allegiance" to their classroom community and all that is important to it.

3. Volunteers may wish to recite their classroom pledges aloud for the rest of the class to hear.

What Do You Do?

• Provide students with a list of names and titles for your community government officials. Encourage students to write a short letter to one of the officials on the list asking a question about his or her job, or a recent task that official accomplished. For example, students may want to know the first thing the new mayor will do when he takes office.

• Suggest that students also summarize in their letters the ways in which they are proud of their community and the work that the government official is doing to help the community meet its needs. You may want to send the letters to the officials and see if they respond. Or, create a classroom exhibit of letters of Community Officials.

What's My Point?

1. Explain to students that there may be more than one point of view on a subject. For example, in the 1200s, King John of England thought it was OK to raise taxes, but the barons did not. The king and the barons had different points of view. Have students suppose that their town or city leaders want to raise their community's taxes, but some people who live in the community do not want to pay higher amounts of money.

2. Ask students to write a paragraph from each side's point of view. For example, the town leaders may want to raise taxes because they think the town's park needs better playground equipment and more flowers. A person in the community might not want to pay higher taxes for this because she is trying to save money to buy a new house.

3. Guide students to organize their paragraphs with a main idea and details to support it. Then have them read their paragraphs aloud. Afterward, others can summarize what they heard.

Pilgrim Poems

The Pilgrims who sailed to Plymouth were a brave group of people. Talk with your students about the Pilgrims' voyage, and what it must have been like to build a new colony in a strange land. If possible, provide reference material for students and invite them to write a short poem or haiku from the point of view of a Pilgrim about his or her experience. Encourage students to illustrate their poems.

Remind students that poems may or may not rhyme, and that a haiku is only three lines of five, seven, and five syllables each. Volunteers can read their poems aloud. Afterward, others can summarize the meaning of the poems.

Citizenship

Caring

When you walk down the street, you can see so many ways that people show they care about their community—from feeding the birds to making sure all the shop windows are sparkling clean!

There are so many ways that people can care for their community. Brainstorm a list of these ways with the class and record it on the chalkboard. Remind students that people can care about the buildings, streets, animals, citizens, trees, and flowers of a community. People can even care about the amount of dirt or noise in the air!

Invite the class to paint a mural that shows all the ways in which people can care for their community. Have students sketch out a miniature plan for their mural before they begin. The entire mural may show Main Street, for example, with people caring for their community in different ways all up and down the street.

After students are satisfied with the final sketch for their mural, have each student paint one or more of the mural sections. Allow students' paintings to dry. If necessary, have students continue painting in another session. Then hang the finished work in a school hallway for all to see and enjoy!

Class Council

OFFICE_____

CANDIDATE_____

OFFICE_____

CANDIDATE_____

OFFICE_____

CANDIDATE_____

OFFICE_____

CANDIDATE_____

OFFICE_____

CANDIDATE_____

OFFICE_____

CANDIDATE_____

OFFICE_____

CANDIDATE_____

OFFICE_____

CANDIDATE_____

Chapter 12 Short-Term Projects

Your students navigate the ins and outs of local government as they make posters, mobiles, and colorful pie charts. Let's get started!

Help Out!
👤 individual 🕐 20 minutes

Materials: poster board, markers or crayons

Ask students to think of a real or made-up school-cleaning project. Then have them create "before" and "after" posters as a way to enlist volunteers for the project. For example, do your classroom windows need to be washed? Students can draw a "before" scene on their poster showing how difficult it is to see through dirty windows, and an "after" scene on the same poster showing students looking at a beautiful, sunny scene through the freshly washed glass.

Suggest that students write catchy phrases on their posters as well. Display the posters in the classroom and have students discuss how this sort of poster might help people get involved in a community project.

"Good Government" Mobile
👥 partners 🕐 30 minutes

Materials: oaktag, scissors, plastic-coated wire hangers, markers or crayons, string, hole-puncher

1. Invite partners to create a colorful mobile. Have them cut out different shapes from oaktag and write an idea about good government on the front and back of each shape. For example: "A good government wants its citizens to know how to read."

2. Then have students color each shape. Model how to use a hole-puncher to make a hole at the top of each shape. Show students how to loop string through the hole and tie the ends around the bottom part of a coat hanger.

3. Guide students to make their strings different lengths so the mobile looks more interesting. Hang students' mobiles around the classroom to help them remember what good government is.

Piece of the Pie

👤 individual   🕐 20 minutes

Materials: chart paper, crayons or markers

Show your students how to draw a pie chart. Model how to divide and label the pie chart into various categories related to government services such as safety and health, education, transportation, and recreation. Ask students to draw their own colorful pie charts. Have them decide how much of their pies each government service should get.

Explain that if a certain service is given a big slice of pie, that service will get more money from the government to pay for it. A big slice of pie for education will mean that there is more money to pay teachers, build schools, and buy school supplies. After students decide how much pie to give to each type of government service, have them write a few sentences explaining their decisions.

Remember! Keep working on that Long-Term Project.

Vice-President Cards

👥 partners   🕐 20 minutes

Materials: index cards, shoebox, crayons or markers, encyclopedias

Who was the first vice-president of the United States? Who is the current vice-president?

1. Write a list of the vice-presidents of the United States on the chalkboard. Have partners choose one or two vice-presidents from the chalkboard list. Then provide students with encyclopedias to help them create fact-file cards.

2. Ask them to draw a picture of the vice-president on the front of the card and label it with the vice-president's name. On the back of the card, have them write facts they discover in their research. For example, the vice-president's date and place of birth, the president he served under, and other important information about his life and work in office.

3. Students who finish early can decorate a shoebox to use as the class fact-file cardholder.

Chapter 12 Writing Projects

Myths and jingles are some of the imaginative writing projects students will tackle as they explore town meetings, the founding of their community, and what they would do if they ruled the world!

"Cleanup" Jingles

Have groups write a jingle about a community cleanup project that could be sung on the radio. Remind students that a jingle is a short song with a catchy melody and that jingles usually promote a service, product, event, or idea. Guide students to first think of a real or possible cleanup project that could happen in their community. For example, is there an abandoned lot that could be turned into a community garden?

Suggest that students set their jingles to a familiar tune, such as "Three Blind Mice." If possible, allow students to record their jingles and play them for the class. Ask them to summarize the idea behind their jingle in one sentence.

Simulation: Public Service Announcement

Come one, come all—to the town meeting! Ask students to write copy for a public service announcement requesting that people attend a town meeting. Remind students that town meetings are public events, usually led by community officials. Often, there is an agenda, or list of topics related to the community that will be discussed.

Suggest that students list the important information they want to include in their announcement before they begin drafting. For example, they probably want to include the date, place, time, and purpose of the town meeting. After students finish writing, have them check over their work to see if there is anything they wish to add or change. Suggest that they make the town meeting sound like an event that no one will want to miss!

TOWN MEETING TODAY! DON'T MISS IT!

The Magic of Myths

Have your students reread the myths "The Founding of Athens" and "The Founding of Rome" on pages 406 and 407 of their textbooks. Remind students that myths are made-up stories involving gods, goddesses, or heroes and their deeds. Then invite students to write a myth about the founding of their community. Have them write a short summary of the plot of their myth before they begin writing. Suggest that they focus on the name of their community in order to get ideas for their myth. Students may also wish to illustrate their myths and share them with the class.

If I Ruled the World

Encourage your students to brainstorm a list of ideas for things they would do or change if they ruled the world. Get creative juices flowing with questions: "Would you make sure everyone got enough to eat? How would you do that? Would you make sure that the environment was respected? How would you do that?"

Ask students to write a summary of the most important things they would do if they ruled the world. If students wish, they may expand on their summaries.

Citizenship

Honesty

Students create special badges to hand out to all the honest people they know. Everyone will want to receive one of these beautiful badges!

Talk with students about the saying "Honesty is the best policy." Have students discuss how honest speech and behavior can help a community. Allow students to speculate on how dishonest speech and behavior can hurt a community.

Invite students to design and create Honesty Badges that they can hand out to people who speak or behave honestly. To make a badge, have students cut a circle or a star shape from oaktag. Ask them to color the badge and write a slogan or phrase on it that says something about honesty. To finish, students can glue or staple small pieces of ribbon onto the back of the badge. Students may wish to make more than one badge to give to all the honest people they know.

Capital Happenings

September
History and Holidays

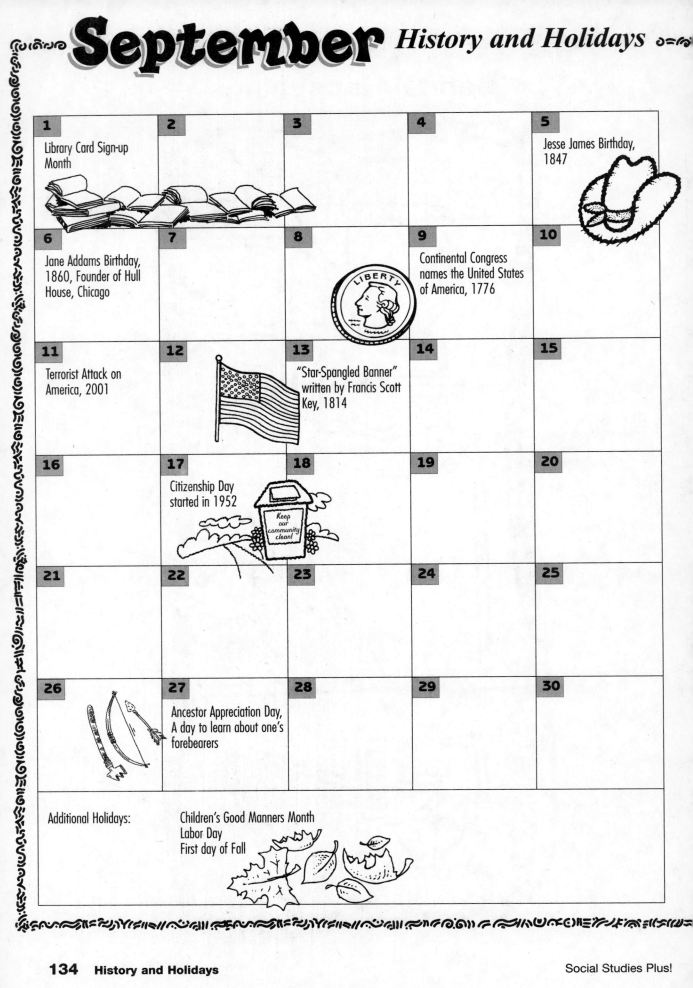

1 Library Card Sign-up Month	**2**	**3**	**4**	**5** Jesse James Birthday, 1847
6 Jane Addams Birthday, 1860, Founder of Hull House, Chicago	**7**	**8**	**9** Continental Congress names the United States of America, 1776	**10**
11 Terrorist Attack on America, 2001	**12**	**13** "Star-Spangled Banner" written by Francis Scott Key, 1814	**14**	**15**
16	**17** Citizenship Day started in 1952	**18**	**19**	**20**
21	**22**	**23**	**24**	**25**
26	**27** Ancestor Appreciation Day, A day to learn about one's forebearers	**28**	**29**	**30**

Additional Holidays:
Children's Good Manners Month
Labor Day
First day of Fall

October
History and Holidays

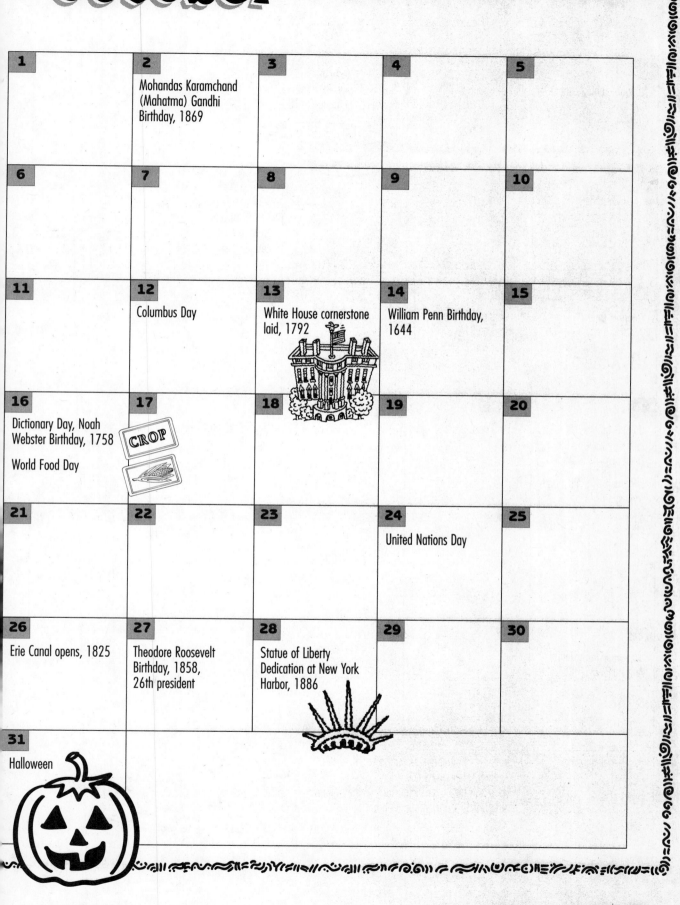

1	**2** Mohandas Karamchand (Mahatma) Gandhi Birthday, 1869	**3**	**4**	**5**
6	**7**	**8**	**9**	**10**
11	**12** Columbus Day	**13** White House cornerstone laid, 1792	**14** William Penn Birthday, 1644	**15**
16 Dictionary Day, Noah Webster Birthday, 1758 World Food Day	**17** CROP	**18**	**19**	**20**
21	**22**	**23**	**24** United Nations Day	**25**
26 Erie Canal opens, 1825	**27** Theodore Roosevelt Birthday, 1858, 26th president	**28** Statue of Liberty Dedication at New York Harbor, 1886	**29**	**30**
31 Halloween				

November History and Holidays

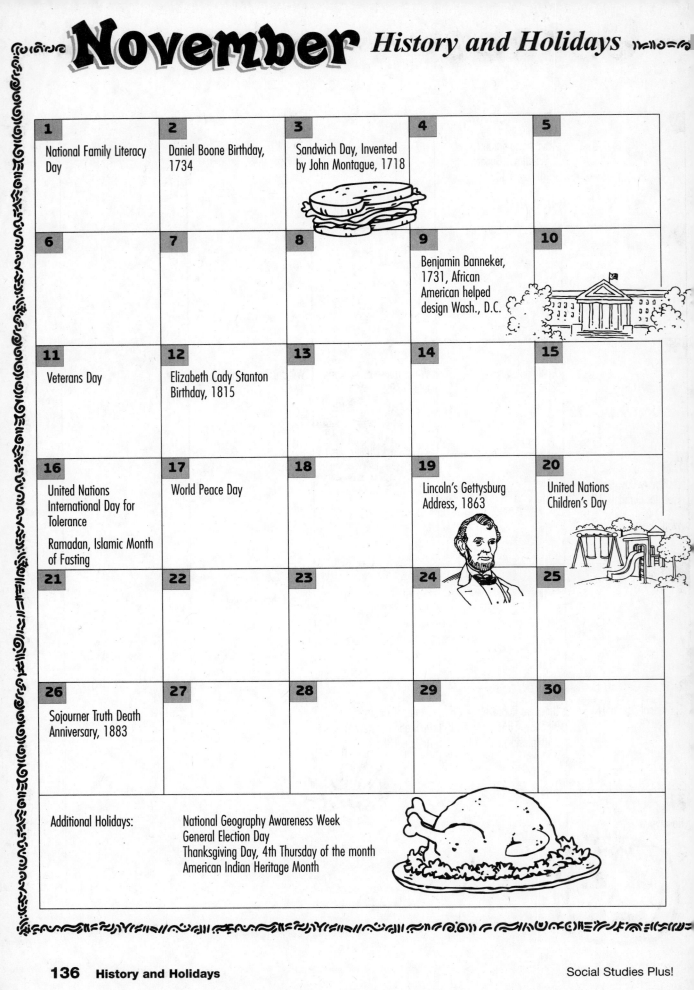

1 National Family Literacy Day	**2** Daniel Boone Birthday, 1734	**3** Sandwich Day, Invented by John Montague, 1718	**4**	**5**
6	**7**	**8**	**9** Benjamin Banneker, 1731, African American helped design Wash., D.C.	**10**
11 Veterans Day	**12** Elizabeth Cady Stanton Birthday, 1815	**13**	**14**	**15**
16 United Nations International Day for Tolerance Ramadan, Islamic Month of Fasting	**17** World Peace Day	**18**	**19** Lincoln's Gettysburg Address, 1863	**20** United Nations Children's Day
21	**22**	**23**	**24**	**25**
26 Sojourner Truth Death Anniversary, 1883	**27**	**28**	**29**	**30**

Additional Holidays:

National Geography Awareness Week
General Election Day
Thanksgiving Day, 4th Thursday of the month
American Indian Heritage Month

Social Studies Plus!

December

History and Holidays

1 Rosa Parks Day, Anniversary of arrest, 1955	**2**	**3**	**4**	**5** Phillis Wheatley Death Anniversary, 1784
6	**7** National Pearl Harbor Remembrance Day, 1941	**8**	**9**	**10** Human Rights Day
11	**12** John Jay Birthday, 1745, First U.S. Supreme Court Chief Justice	**13**	**14**	**15** Bill of Rights Day Sitting Bull Death Anniversary, 1890
16 Boston Tea Party, 1773	**17**	**18**	**19**	**20**
21 Pilgrim landing at Plymouth Rock, 1620	**22**	**23**	**24**	**25**
26	**27**	**28** Pledge of Allegiance recognized, 1945 *Poor Richard's Almanack,* by Richard Saunders (a.k.a. Benjamin Franklin)	**29**	**30**
31	Additional Holidays:	First day of Winter		

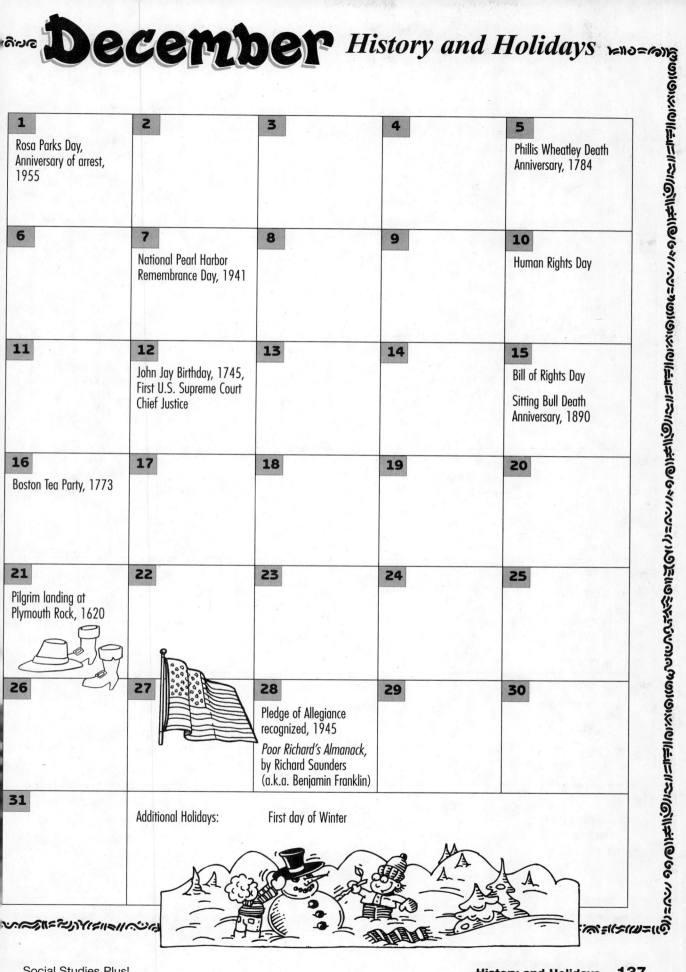

January History and Holidays

1 Paul Revere Birthday, 1735 Betsy Ross Birthday, 1752 New Year's Day	**2**	**3**	**4**	**5** George Washington Carver Death Anniversary, 1943
6	**7**	**8** Universal Letter Writing Week 	**9**	**10**
11	**12**	**13**	**14**	**15** Martin Luther King, Jr. Birthday, 1929
16	**17** Benjamin Franklin Birthday, 1706	**18**	**19** Robert E. Lee Birthday, 1807, Confederate leader	**20**
21 Do Something: Kindness & Justice Challenge Ethan Allen Birthday, 1738, "Green Mountain Boys" leader	**22**	**23** School Nurse Day National Compliment Day (compliment at least 5 people)	**24** California gold discovered in Sutter's Creek, 1848	**25**
26	**27**	**28** Challenger Space Shuttle Explosion, 1986 (11:39 A.M.)	**29**	**30**
31 Jackie Robinson Birthday, 1919, First African American in major league baseball	Additional Holidays: Lee-Jackson-King Day, (Virginia)			

1 Langston Hughes Birthday, 1902	**2** Groundhog Day	**3**	**4** Charles Lindbergh, Birthday, 1902, First to fly solo across the Atlantic	**5**
6 "Babe" Ruth Birthday, 1895	**7**	**8**	**9**	**10**
11 Thomas Alva Edison Birthday, 1847	**12** Abraham Lincoln Birthday, 1809	**13**	**14** Valentine's Day	**15**
16	**17**	**18**	**19**	**20**
21	**22** George Washington Birthday, 1732	**23**	**24**	**25**
26	**27**	**28**		

Additional Holidays: Presidents' Day
African American History Month

March *History and Holidays*

1	2	3	4	5
				Boston Massacre, 1770

6	7	8	9	10
Fall of the Alamo, 1836, in present-day San Antonio				Harriet Tubman Death Anniversary, 1913, Leader, Underground Railroad First telephone call, 1876, by Alexander Graham Bell

11	12	13	14	15
				Ides of March (Julius Caesar assassinated, 44 B.C.)

16	17	18	19	20
	Saint Patrick's Day			

21	22	23	24	25
	First women's collegiate basketball game, 1893	Liberty Day		

26	27	28	29	30

31				
	Additional Holidays:	First day of Spring Women's History Month		

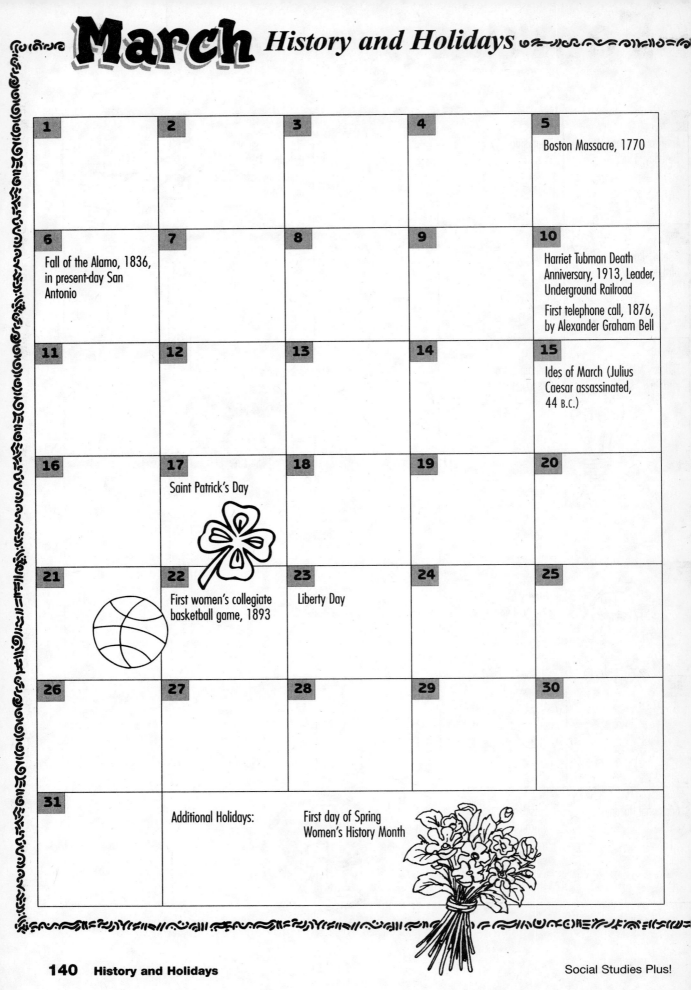

April
History and Holidays

1 April Fools' Day	**2** International Children's Book Day	**3**	**4**	**5**
6	**7**	**8** Ryan White Death Anniversary, AIDS activist	**9**	**10**
11 Civil Rights Act of 1968	**12** Polio Vaccine, 1955, Developed by Dr. Jonas E. Salk First Space Shuttle flight, Columbia, 1981	**13** Thomas Jefferson Birthday, 1743	**14** Moment of Laughter Day	**15**
16	**17**	**18** Paul Revere's "Midnight Ride," 1775	**19**	**20**
21	**22** Earth Day	**23**	**24**	**25** Take Our Daughters and Sons To Work Day
26 Arbor Day, National day for planting trees	**27** Ulysses Simpson Grant Birthday, 1822, 18th president	**28**	**29**	**30**

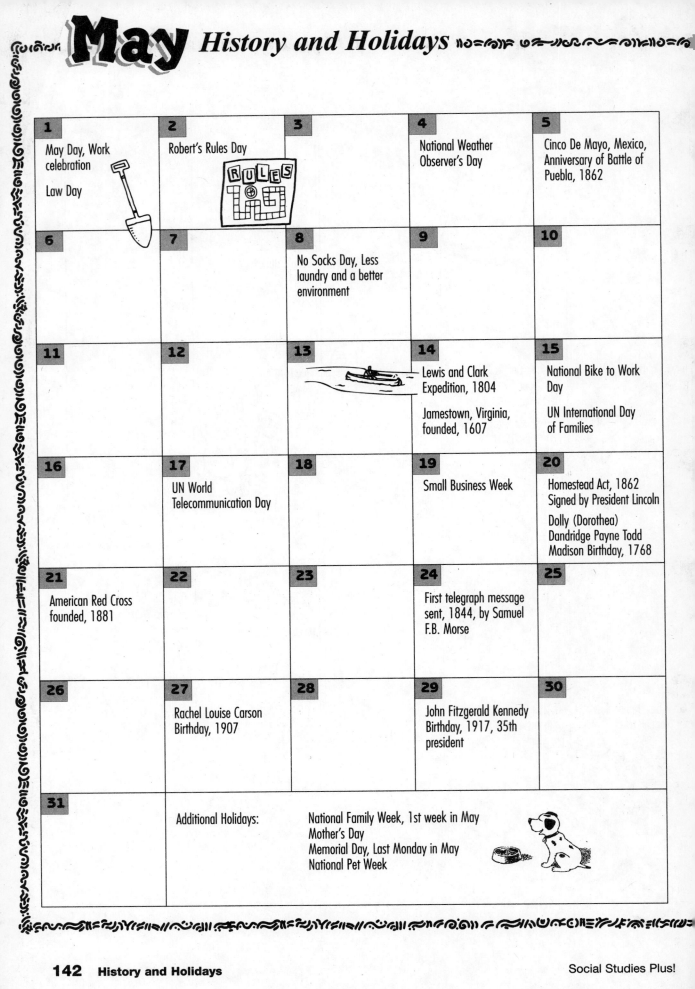

1	2	3	4	5
May Day, Work celebration Law Day	Robert's Rules Day		National Weather Observer's Day	Cinco De Mayo, Mexico, Anniversary of Battle of Puebla, 1862
6	**7**	**8** No Socks Day, Less laundry and a better environment	**9**	**10**
11	**12**	**13**	**14** Lewis and Clark Expedition, 1804 Jamestown, Virginia, founded, 1607	**15** National Bike to Work Day UN International Day of Families
16	**17** UN World Telecommunication Day	**18**	**19** Small Business Week	**20** Homestead Act, 1862 Signed by President Lincoln Dolly (Dorothea) Dandridge Payne Todd Madison Birthday, 1768
21 American Red Cross founded, 1881	**22**	**23**	**24** First telegraph message sent, 1844, by Samuel F.B. Morse	**25**
26	**27** Rachel Louise Carson Birthday, 1907	**28**	**29** John Fitzgerald Kennedy Birthday, 1917, 35th president	**30**

31

Additional Holidays:
National Family Week, 1st week in May
Mother's Day
Memorial Day, Last Monday in May
National Pet Week

June History and Holidays

1	**2**	**3** Jefferson Davis Birthday, 1808	**4**	**5**
6 D-Day Anniversary, 1944	**7** VCR introduced, 1975	**8**	**9** Donald Duck Birthday, 1934	**10** Ball-point pen patented, 1943
11 Jacques Cousteau Birthday, 1910	**12**	**13**	**14** Flag Day, Proclaimed 1916 — Harriet Beecher Stowe Birthday, 1811, *Uncle Tom's Cabin* author	**15**
16	**17**	**18** Dr. Sally Ride, First American woman in space, 1983	**19** Juneteenth, 1868, News of the Emancipation Proclamation reached Texas	**20**
21	**22**	**23**	**24**	**25**
26	**27** "Happy Birthday To You" composed, 1859 — Helen Keller Birthday, 1880	**28**	**29**	**30**

Additional Holidays: Father's Day
First day of Summer

July *History and Holidays*

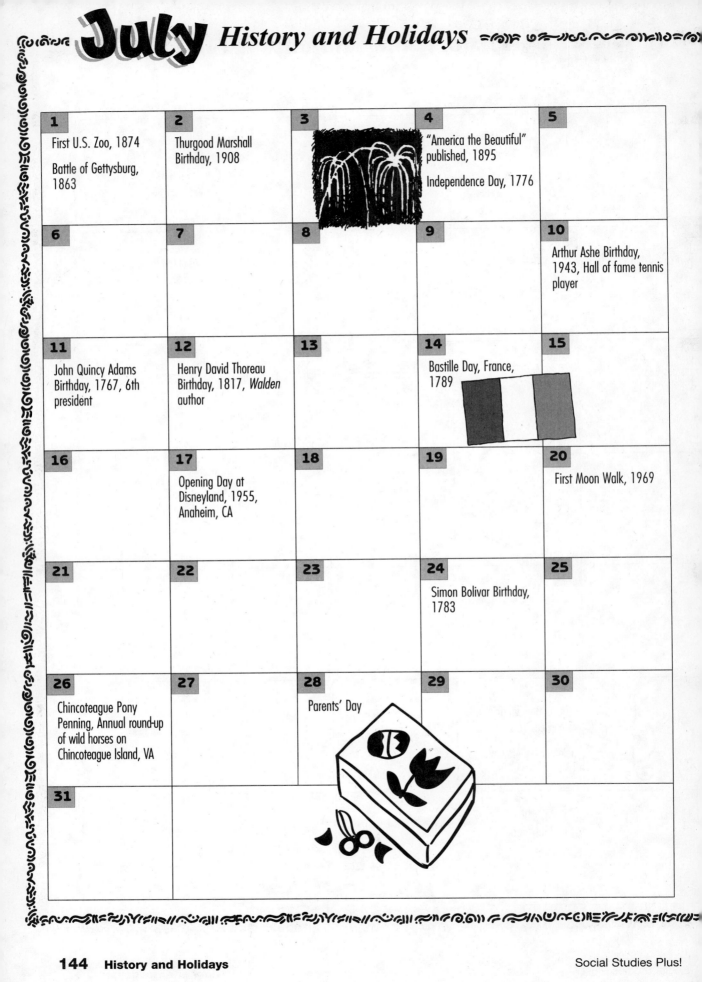

1 First U.S. Zoo, 1874 Battle of Gettysburg, 1863	**2** Thurgood Marshall Birthday, 1908	**3**	**4** "America the Beautiful" published, 1895 Independence Day, 1776	**5**
6	**7**	**8**	**9**	**10** Arthur Ashe Birthday, 1943, Hall of fame tennis player
11 John Quincy Adams Birthday, 1767, 6th president	**12** Henry David Thoreau Birthday, 1817, *Walden* author	**13**	**14** Bastille Day, France, 1789	**15**
16	**17** Opening Day at Disneyland, 1955, Anaheim, CA	**18**	**19**	**20** First Moon Walk, 1969
21	**22**	**23**	**24** Simon Bolivar Birthday, 1783	**25**
26 Chincoteague Pony Penning, Annual round-up of wild horses on Chincoteague Island, VA	**27**	**28** Parents' Day	**29**	**30**
31				

August History and Holidays

1	**2**	**3**	**4**	**5** Sisters' Day
6 Jamaica Independence Day	**7** First picture of Earth taken from outer space	**8**	**9**	**10**
11 Frederick Douglass first speaks as a free man, 1841	**12**	**13** Annie Oakley Birthday, 1860, Star of Buffalo Bill's Wild West Show	**14**	**15**
16	**17** David "Davy" Crockett Birthday, 1786	**18** Virginia Dare Birthday, 1587, First English child born in the New World	**19**	**20**
21	**22**	**23**	**24**	**25**
26	**27** Lyndon B. Johnson Birthday, 1908, 36th president	**28**	**29**	**30**
31				

NOTES

NOTES

NOTES